Terry Pratchett's

HOGFATHER

The Illustrated Screenplay

Terry Pratchett,
Vadim Jean,

Bill Kaye

&

Stephen Player

ALSO BY TERRY PRATCHETT

THE CARPET PEOPLE
THE DARK SIDE OF THE SUN
STRATA
TRUCKERS
DIGGERS
WINGS
ONLY YOU CAN SAVE MANKIND
JOHNNY AND THE DEAD
JOHNNY AND THE BOMB
THE UNADULTERATED CAT (with Gray Jolliffe)
GOOD OMENS (with Neil Gaiman)

The Discworld® Series:
THE COLOUR OF MAGIC
THE LIGHT FANTASTIC
EQUAL RITES
MORT
SOURCERY
WYRD SISTERS
PYRAMIDS
GUARDS! GUARDS!
ERIC (with Josh Kirby)
MOVING PICTURES
REAPER MAN
WITCHES ABROAD
SMALL GODS
LORDS AND LADIES
MEN AT ARMS
SOUL MUSIC
INTERESTING TIMES
MASKERADE
FEET OF CLAY
HOGFATHER
JINGO
THE LAST CONTINENT
CARPE JUGULUM
THE FIFTH ELEPHANT
THE TRUTH
THE THIEF OF TIME
THE LAST HERO
(with Paul Kidby)
NIGHT WATCH
MONSTROUS REGIMENT
GOING POSTAL
THUD!
MAKING MONEY

THE AMAZING MAURICE AND HIS EDUCATED
RODENTS
WEE FREE MEN
A HATFUL OF SKY
WINTERSMITH
WHERE'S MY COW?
MORT: A DISCWORLD BIG COMIC
(with Graham Higgins)
GUARDS! GUARDS! (with Graham Higgins)
THE PRATCHETT PORTFOLIO (with Paul Kidby)
THE DISCWORLD COMPANION (with Stephen Briggs)
THE STREETS OF ANKH-MORPORK
(with Stephen Briggs)
THE DISCWORLD MAPP (with Stephen Briggs)
A TOURIST GUIDE TO LANCRE:
A DISCWORLD MAPP
(with Stephen Briggs and Paul Kidby)
DEATH'S DOMAIN (with Paul Kidby)
NANNY OGG'S COOKBOOK
THE WIT AND WISDOM OF DISCWORLD
(with Stephen Briggs)
THE DISCWORLD'S UNSEEN
UNIVERSITY DIARY 1998
(with Stephen Briggs and Paul Kidby)
THE DISCWORLD'S ANKH-MORPORK CITY
WATCH DIARY 1999
(with Stephen Briggs and Paul Kidby)
THE DISCWORLD ASSASSINS' GUILD DIARY 2000
(with Stephen Briggs and Paul Kidby)
THE DISCWORLD FOOLS' GUILD YEARBOOK
AND DIARY 2001
(with Stephen Briggs and Paul Kidby)
THE DISCWORLD THIEVES' GUILD YEARBOOK
AND DIARY 2002
(with Stephen Briggs and Paul Kidby)
THE DISCWORLD (REFORMED) VAMPYRE'S
DIARY 2003
(with Stephen Briggs and Paul Kidby)
THE ANKH-MORPORK POST OFFICE
HANDBOOK AND DIARY 2007
(with Stephen Briggs and Paul Kidby)
LU-TZE'S YEARBOOK OF ENLIGHTENMENT 2008
(with Stephen Briggs and Paul Kidby)
THE NEW DISCWORLD COMPANION
(with Stephen Briggs)

Terry Pratchett's

HOGFATHER

The Illustrated Screenplay

First published in Great Britain in 2006 by Gollancz
This edition published in Great Britain in 2007 by Gollancz
A subsidiary of the Orion Publishing Group
Orion House, 5 Upper St Martin's Lane, London WC2H 9EA

A CIP catalogue record for this book is available
from the British Library

ISBN 978 0 57508 0 393

1 3 5 7 9 10 8 6 4 2

Printed and bound in Italy.

www.orionbooks.co.uk

The Orion Publishing Group's policy is to use papers that are natural,
renewable and recyclable products and made from wood grown in sustainable forests.
The logging and manufacturing processes are expected to conform to the
environmental regulations of the country of origin.

FOREWORD
BY TERRY PRATCHETT

Walking around inside my own head

It was the shoes that did it for me. They looked like something Edmund Blackadder had thrown away quite hard. They were right for the period, I was advised, but since the setting was Discworld we had to decide on what period we meant, which we ultimately agreed was Late Georgian without the Late George.

The hat and shirt changed around. My own glasses were swapped for something more antique, but the shoes, by common consent, stayed. And, as I tried them on, I thought, Good grief, this might actually happen! And if they're taking this much trouble over a pair of old shoes, it might actually be done well!

I played the Toymaker, a small but important part that required me to be scared most of the time. Since I spend most of that time face to er . . . face with Death, this was not hard. And, just to ease me gently into my thespianic debut, mine was the first scene on the first day of the shooting of *Hogfather: The Movie*.

And it did happen, and they did take the trouble.

Movies often don't happen. It is their ground state of being. They run the gamut of people with no power to say yes but lots of power to say no, until you believe that movies get made only because people have run out of excuses not to. And then, as one exasperated producer once put it to me, 'When you've convinced all the Treens, they go and change the Mekon.'

But this one got off the ground after quite a pleasant trip down the runway, and, as I saw the development of the script and the storyboards and the sets and the cast list, it began to fly and took me with it. They'd got it, all the way to the top. They knew how it should go, and they were still confident enough to include me in from the script onwards.

We talked about the look of the city of Ankh-Morpork, which had to be 'real' – real bricks, real dirt, real colours. Fantasy isn't the same as weird

. . . but London has its secret share of fantasy places, if you have the knowing of such things, and The Mob found them out. It's amazing how ingenuity can do the work of money.

We discussed actors and they got me David Warner as Lord Downey, for example. They also said: 'We've got Michelle Dockery to play Susan. Trust us – she *is* Susan.' And she was. (The other scene on the first day was of Michelle riding the giant hog. During a break, she was kind enough to tell me how well her costume fitted. It's these little details that you cherish . . .)

And I learned the verb 'to snot'. How did I ever manage without it? It's a rather more versatile form of 'to distress', and is the art of making new places and items look as though they are a hundred years old and have been sorely mistreated every day. There's some wonderful snotting in *Hogfather*.

Then they started sending me the rushes, and it was as if all my Hogswatches had come at once.

I talk about it as if it was all for me, but that's how it can feel like, as you walk through the very disorientating tower of the Tooth Fairy or feel the incredibly realistic snow of the Hogfather's Castle of Bones crunch underfoot. Oh, you know, in a vague kind of way, that there are people out there, at the other end of the process, and you also know that even a three-hour movie means that there are good lines and cherished scenes that never even made it as far as the cutting-room floor, but surely the art is to prune or cut away all those pieces that don't fit or aren't needed any more and still leave the soul intact. If you can make an author get the weird sensation that he is walking around the inside of his own head, then you're probably doing it right.

It was fun.

And now it turns out that it wasn't all for me, but for you, too.

Terry Pratchett
Creator

FOREWORD
BY VADIM JEAN

Everything starts somewhere. In my case it was Heathrow Airport . . . in the limbo of Departure Lounge Delay without a book. And as I passed the shelf of Pratchetts, stretching off into apparent infinity, something told me that I could resist no longer. Fatefully, from the depths of my memory I recalled a time ten years ago, when my friend Nigel Planer had been forced to postpone his dubbing session for one of my movies as he'd lost his voice after a week of reading unabridged Discworld audio books. If Nigel was prepared to lose his voice for Terry Pratchett, then there had to be something in it.

I didn't stop laughing out loud until, somewhere over Greenland and much to the relief of my fellow passengers, I put *The Colour of Magic* down.

And from the moment Rincewind looked back down over Ankh-Morpork in flames with Twoflower's luggage at his feet and a seven-foot skeleton with the scythe, the robes and the CAPITALISED DIALOGUE had made an appearance, I knew this world had to be in a movie.

Waxing (or as I now realise, Weatherwaxing) lyrical at my desk about my new discovery, I was about to owe a debt of gratitude to James Graham with whom I share an office – for not only does he have a brain the size of a planet, but he's also read every single Discworld novel. Eager to know which book I should read next, he said that now momentous word: *Hogfather*. For your inspiration, James, I shall be forever grateful.

With its sparklingly witty dialogue, fantastic comedic premise (how can Death standing in for Discworld's sort-of Father Christmas not tickle your stocking?), *Hogfather* made me want to read every book in the series. But, most of all, it confirmed what *The Colour of Magic* had started to make me think: that here was what I was born to bring to the screen.

The film industry being what it is, another few years passed before the strange mixture of chance, opportunity, good fortune and timing coincided to make this dream become a possibility. Naturally enough, it started with a meeting about another project entirely. I was supposed to be at their offices in Isleworth for our first meeting with Sky. So, while producers Rod Brown and

Ian Sharples were being thoroughly professional, on time and actually there with the Head of Drama, *I* was fifteen miles away in Soho, at entirely the wrong venue. I had never before met the Sky executives, so I must have made a really great first impression – but somehow, on the other end of a mobile phone, and no doubt smoothed by great producing, I did. Most importantly, the Head of Drama said the immortal words: 'What we really want is a sci-fi/fantasy franchise.'

I said the magic words: 'Terry Pratchett'. No one else had yet done it, so my ambition to be the first to bring a live-action adaptation of a Discworld novel to the screen was still possible. You can only dream about the Head of the Channel turning out to be a Pratchett fan – and that was exactly what the visionary James Baker was! The rest, to misquote something somebody somewhere is alleged to have said, will perhaps one day be history.

The combination of a clear idea of how we wanted to treat the book, a trip to Wincanton for Hogswatch, and producer Rod's legendary powers of persuasion helped Terry to recognise that we didn't just want an option on a *property*; we wanted to actually *tell* the story.

So now all that remained was the simple task of adapting the work of a genius . . .

Not having personally written any of the six feature films I've directed meant I was entirely insane – or at least delirious – when I decided that I wanted to do the adaptation myself. Whichever it turned out to be (and you may now, thanks to Gollancz, judge for yourself) the equally barmy producers agreed. They also agreed to the appointment of Phil Parker as script editor. Over the years I've learned more about screenplay writing from Phil than from anyone else, and his contribution to the daunting task of restructuring the interweaving stories and complex ideas of *Hogfather* was immense.

One of the things I'd always loved about Terry's writing is that it was so visual, so cinematic, and I also felt much of the dialogue should remain unchanged. Above all, I wanted to be truly faithful to the book. I wanted to be able to watch the finished film two years after the first word was written and see the book on the screen, exactly as I had imagined it from reading the text. I loved the novel so much that, frankly, I wouldn't have cared if not a single word was mine and all I'd had to do was edit what was already there. And the last thing I wanted was a screenwriter with an ego, someone who wanted to make it theirs. It's Terry Pratchett's *Hogfather* for a reason.

So my big question was: would I be able to find Terry's voice in the words that I would be shaping to bring to the screen his incredible vision of Discworld? As the development process began, I faced the inevitable challenges of having to lose several of my favourite parts of the novel for the sake of the story. I wish I'd had enough screen time for the King to give his leftovers to the peasant happy with his beany lot, and for muddy boots to be served in the restaurant. If your favourite scene or character is not included, I apologise, even if it is the God of Indigestion (against whom I have a particular gripe anyway, and so exacted an editorial revenge). But something has to give, even in the four hours that television has given us to tell the story.

So it was with trepidation that I awaited Terry's response to the first draft of the screenplay. It was with joy and relief that I greeted his first comment: 'Most of the words seem to be mine . . .' As a humble adapter, that was exactly what I wanted to hear, and that reassurance was confirmed when Colin Smythe said that Terry *wanted to give me some notes* . . .

And so, on a wonderfully sunny day in the West Country, I had the honour of a day of Terry's time, during which he made suggestions of humour, faithfulness to Discworld and yet more invention: my adaptation was 'Mucked About With' to perfection by the Creator himself. The moment when Terry said of one particular speech that even if he hadn't written it, he wished he had, will remain one of the proudest of my life – because it was one of mine. Sometime during that eight months immersed in *Hogfather* I had found a smidgeon of Terry's own voice in my own writing.

There are many people to thank who have made tremendous contributions to this adaptation, but in particular: Terry (for everything), Phil Parker, who is the best script doctor in Britain (and whose beard played a major part in convincing Terry he wasn't a suit), Elaine Pyke, our Commissioning Editor and Sarah Conroy at Sky, Lyn Holst at RHI, Rod and Ian for brilliant producing, and, most of all, my wife Susan for letting me live in Discworld for two years.

Happy Hogswatch!

Vadim Jean
Writer/Director Hogfather

Terry Pratchett's
HOGFATHER
The Illustrated Screenplay

PART ONE

WRITTEN FOR THE SCREEN

BY VADIM JEAN

MUCKED AROUND WITH

BY TERRY PRATCHETT

EXT. SPACE – NIGHT

Mists roll, stars peek, glinting faintly through.

> NARRATOR (VOICE OVER)
> Everything starts somewhere, although
> many physicists disagree. There is the
> constant desire to find out where.
> Where is the point where it all began?

A star explodes, and in the distance we can just make
out an odd shape. We fly towards the Discworld.

> NARRATOR (V.O.)
> But much, much later than that, the
> Discworld was formed . . .

We fly around the Turtle, and the Discworld.

> NARRATOR (V.O.)
> . . . drifting onwards through
> space atop four elephants on
> the shell of a giant turtle,
> The Great A'Tuin.

We begin to fly over the Discworld.

> NARRATOR (V.O.)
> It was some time after its creation
> when most people forgot that the very
> oldest stories of the beginning are,
> sooner or later, about blood . . .

And now we're flying across the disc itself.

> NARRATOR (V.O.)
> . . . at least that's one theory . . . the
> philosopher Didactylos has suggested an
> alternative hypothesis: 'Things just
> happen. What the hell.'

And onwards over the city and down towards the centre . . .

> NARRATOR (V.O.)
> And so our story begins in Ankh-
> Morpork, the twin city of proud Ankh
> and pestilent Morpork, the biggest city
> in Discworld . . .

We fly over the city to the Tower of Art.

                    NARRATOR (V.O.)
        A city where magic is just another job,
        and where the Tower of Art of the
        Unseen University for Wizards looms
        over all the dark narrow streets.

And plummet to the street below.

                    NARRATOR (V.O.)
        Our story begins on a midwinter
        festival bearing a remarkable
        similarity to your Christmas.

                    NARRATOR (V.O.)

And so . . .

EXT. GAITER'S HOUSE – NIGHT

We travel over the rooftops of Ankh-Morpork.

                    NARRATOR (V.O.)
        . . . It was the night before Hogswatch . . .

The glow of candlelight draws us towards one of the
windows in a Georgian looking house. As the CAMERA
cranes closer we hear over . . .

                    SUSAN (Off Camera)
        . . . and then Jack chopped down what
        was the world's last beanstalk, adding
        murder and ecological terrorism to the
        theft, enticement and trespass charges
        already mentioned . . .

INT. GAITER'S HOUSE/TWYLA'S BEDROOM – NIGHT

SUSAN STO-HELIT is reading a bedtime story to two small
children, TWYLA and GAWAIN. They are about seven and
five years old respectively.

On the cover we see the title: *Jack and the Beanstalk*.

                    SUSAN
        . . . and all the giant's children
        didn't have a daddy any more . . . but
        he got away with it and lived happily
        ever after without so much as a guilty
        twinge about what he had done.

The children are listening contentedly just their eyes peeking over the covers.

                    SUSAN
          Which proves that you can be excused
          just about anything if you're a hero,
          because no one asks inconvenient
          questions. And now . . .

Susan closes the book with a snap.

                    SUSAN
          . . . it's time for bed.

                    TWYLA
     Susan?

                    SUSAN
     Yes?

                    TWYLA
     You know last week when we
     wrote a letter to the
     Hogfather?

                    SUSAN
     Yes.

                    TWYLA
     Well, will he really come?

There is a rustle from the other bed. Twyla's brother, Gawain, turns over to listen surreptitiously.

                    GAWAIN
          And when's he coming here?

Susan sits down on the bed, wondering how the hell to get through this. She pats Twyla's one visible hand and takes a deep mental breath.

                    SUSAN
          Does it matter if you get the
          presents anyway?

                    TWYLA
     Yes.

14

It obviously does matter. Susan tries another tack.

> SUSAN
> Well, if you don't believe in the
> Hogfather, there won't be any presents.

> TWYLA
> Fawt so.

Susan taps Twyla's hand and finishes tucking her in.

And with that the CAMERA pulls back through the window.

> NARRATOR (V.O.)

> But while children everywhere sleep
> fitfully in the belief that a jolly fat
> man is about to deliver their presents,
> not necessarily everyone is entering
> the Hogswatch spirit.

EXT. GUILD OF ASSASSINS - NIGHT

The CAMERA flies towards a public school-like building
and glides finally to rest at the engraved brass plaque
by its gate . . . the GUILD OF ASSASSINS.

> NARRATOR (V.O.)

> Especially in a city where there is a
> Guild for everything.

INT. GUILD OF ASSASSINS - NIGHT

A modest brass plaque is screwed into a wall next to a
wooden picture frame, bearing the comment 'Departed
this vale of tears on Grune 3, Year of the Sideways
Leech, with the assistance of the Hon. K. W. Dobson.'

As the CAMERA pulls out we see that we are in a wood-
panelled corridor where a number of paintings and busts
of the famous clients of members of the guild line the
walls.

We arrive at a distinguished-looking door with an
important-looking plaque: LORD DOWNEY: MASTER OF THE
GUILD.

INT. LORD DOWNEY'S STUDY - NIGHT

LORD DOWNEY sits in his study catching up on the paperwork.

The study is oak-panelled and well carpeted. The furniture is very old and quite worn.

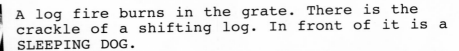

A log fire burns in the grate. There is the crackle of a shifting log. In front of it is a SLEEPING DOG.

There is no other sound but the scratching of Lord Downey's pen and the ticking of the longcase clock by the door . . . until . . . someone clears their throat.

Downey stops writing but does not raise his head.

He considers for a moment.

> LORD DOWNEY
> (businesslike)
> The doors are locked, the windows are barred, the dog does not appear to have woken up, the squeaky floorboards haven't. I really doubt that you are a ghost, and gods generally do not announce themselves so politely. You could, of course, be Death, but I don't believe he bothers with such niceties. Besides, I'm feeling quite well.

And then he looks up.

One of the AUDITORS hangs in the air.

> LORD DOWNEY
> Good evening.

> AUDITOR 1
> Good evening, Lord Downey.

> LORD DOWNEY
> You appear to be a spectre.

> AUDITOR 1
> Our nature is not a matter for discussion. We offer you a commission.

                    LORD DOWNEY
        You wish someone inhumed?

                    AUDITOR 1
        Brought to an end.

Downey considers for a moment.

                    LORD DOWNEY
        Our scale of fees . . .

                    AUDITOR 1
        The payment will be three
        million dollars.

Downey sits back trying
unsuccessfully to hide his surprise
at the enormity of the sum.

                    LORD DOWNEY
        No questions asked, I assume?

                    AUDITOR 1
        No questions answered.

                    LORD DOWNEY
        But does the suggested fee
        represent the difficulty
        involved? The client is heavily
        guarded?

                    AUDITOR 1
        Not guarded at all. But almost
        certainly impossible to delete
        with conventional weapons.

Downey nods, thinking for a moment.

                    LORD DOWNEY
        We like to know for whom we are
        working.

                    AUDITOR 1
        We are sure you do.

                    LORD DOWNEY
        We need to know your name. Or names.
        In strict client confidentiality, of
        course.

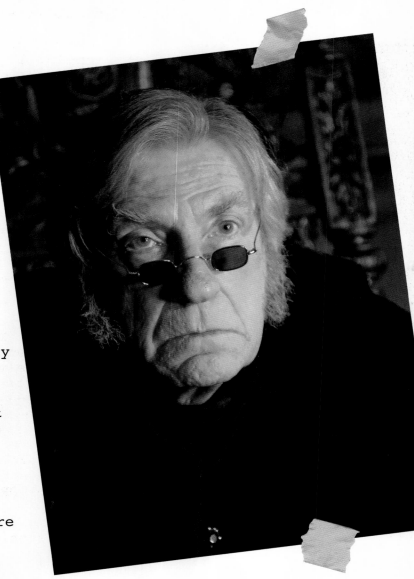

                    AUDITOR 1
          You may think of us as . . . the
          Auditors.

                    LORD DOWNEY
          Really? What do you audit?

                    AUDITOR 1
          Everything . . . We maintain the logical
          order of the universe.

                    LORD DOWNEY
          I think we need to know a little more
          than that—

                    AUDITOR 1
          We are the people with three million
          dollars.

Downey takes the point.

                    LORD DOWNEY
          We will need to know where, when and,
          of course, who.

The cowl nods.

                    AUDITOR 1
          The location is not on any map, and we
          need the task to be completed by
          sunrise tomorrow. This is essential. As
          for the who . . .

A DRAWING appears on Downey's desk.

                    AUDITOR 1
          Let us call him the Fat Man.

                    LORD DOWNEY
          But won't he be out on his rounds?

INTERIOR HOUSE–DISCWORLD - NIGHT

The room is brightly decorated. Ivy and mistletoe hang
in bunches from the bookshelves. Brightly coloured
streamers festoon the walls.

At one end there is a classic Victorian style fireside.
In the grate a fire has died down to a few sullen
ashes.

Hanging from the mantelpiece are a couple of
long stockings. Ranged along it is a
selection of cards. They have messages like
'Wishing you Joye and all Goode Cheer at
Hogswatchtime & All Through The Yeare' on
them.

A RED-CLOAKED FIGURE pulls itself
upright and looks around the room.

It is the HOGFATHER.

He moves in a very jolly fashion to a
large leather armchair with a table
by its side.

On the table is a GLASS OF SHERRY,
a PORK PIE and four TURNIPS. There
is also a note. The Hogfather
reads . . .

> *Dere Hogfather,*
>
> *For Hogswatch I would like a toy
> soldier, a drum and red and white candy
> cane an here is a glars of Sherre an a Pork
> pie for you and turnips for Gouger an Rooter
> an Snot Snouter.*

The Hogfather fills the stockings
hanging above the mantelpiece: a
teddy bear, a toy soldier in a
colourful uniform, a drum and a red-
and-white candy cane.

He sips the sherry, pockets both the pork pie
and the turnips and then goes back over to the fire.

Then, as he swings the sack back over his shoulder we
see his face for the first time. It is a beamingly
jolly face, half man, half hog.

                    HOGFATHER
          Ho ho ho.

And with that he ducks down, enters the chimney and
with a magical whooshing sound is gone.

INT. LORD DOWNEY'S STUDY - NIGHT

                    LORD DOWNEY
            Is this a joke?

                    AUDITOR 1
            We have no sense of humour.

Downey drums his fingers.

                    LORD DOWNEY
            There are some who say this ...
            person does not exist.

                    AUDITOR 1
            He must exist. How else could
            you so readily recognise his
            picture?

Downey looks at the drawing again. It's
of . . . the HOGFATHER.

                    AUDITOR 1
            And many are in correspondence
            with him.

He has a point.

                    LORD DOWNEY
            He would be difficult to find.

                    AUDITOR 1
            You will find persons on any street who
            can tell you his approximate address.

                    LORD DOWNEY
            Yes, of course, but, as you say, they
            can hardly give a map reference. Even
            then, how would the . . . Fat Man be
            inhumed? A glass of poisoned sherry,
            perhaps?

The cowl has no face to crack a smile.

                    AUDITOR 1
            You misunderstand the nature of
            employment.

                    LORD DOWNEY
                (sniffily)
            How do I misunderstand you, exactly?

AUDITOR 1
We pay. You find the ways and means.

LORD DOWNEY
How can I contact you?

AUDITOR 1
We will contact you. We know where you
are. We know where everyone is.

The figure vanishes.

Downey stares into space for a while, and then smiles.
He picks up a speaker tube by his desk.

LORD DOWNEY
Winvoe.

WINVOE
Yes sir. What is it, sir?

LORD DOWNEY
Is Mister Teatime still in the building?

Downey picks up the picture of the Hogfather from his
desk and looks at it thoughtfully.

EXTERIOR HOUSE-DISCWORLD/ROOF - NIGHT

The Hogfather's sleigh is ancient and runs on what look
like two felled trees side by side with the branches
still attached. By his side is a tiny, immaculately
dressed PIXIE with a perfect smile. The HOGFATHER snaps
the reins.

HOGFATHER
Up, Gouger! Up, Rooter! Up, Tusker! Up,
Snouter! Giddyup!

PIXIE
Wey hey!

The HOGS lurch forward and the sleigh
flies off into the night. Snow
begins to fall into the PERFECT
SLEIGH TRACKS left on the roof.

EXT. GAITER'S HOUSE/SUSAN'S BEDROOM - NIGHT

Frost patterns curl across the glass. As we get closer, within we start to make out

INT. GAITER'S HOUSE/SUSAN'S BEDROOM - NIGHT

Susan. She is sitting up on the bed, reading by candlelight.

A tapping sound on the window makes her turn her head.

Just visible through the frost is a BLACK BEAK tapping hard at the glass.

Susan looks abruptly away.

> SUSAN
> Go away! I don't do that stuff anymore!

She blinks . . . then turns back to the window.

The sound of wings clatter against the glass as the DARK OUTLINE of a BLACK BIRD flies away, its shadow whipping across the window sill and then disappearing.

Susan sighs and looks around.

> At her door TWYLA stands barefoot in a nightdress. She looks ridiculously cute in the slightly oversize garment.

> SUSAN
> (Sighing)
> Yes, Twyla?

> TWYLA
> I'm afwaid of the monster in the cellar, Thusan. It's going to eat me up.

Susan shuts her book firmly.

> SUSAN
> What, again? Oh.

Susan gets off the bed, trying to stay quite calm.

Twyla watches her.

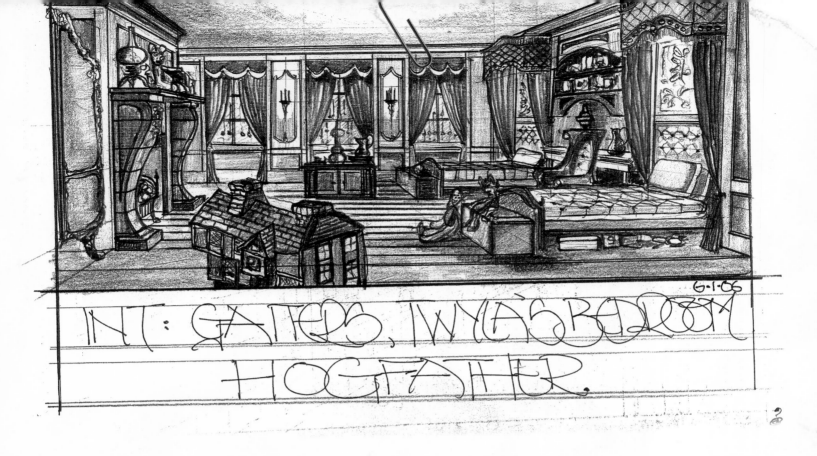

INT. GAITERS, TWYLA'S BEDROOM
HOGFATHER.

Susan picks up the poker from the nursery fender and leaves.

INT. GAITER'S HOUSE/BACK STAIRS – NIGHT

SUSAN goes down the back stairs, with TWYLA following her. We hear muffled voices coming from the direction of the dining room. As they creep past, the door opens.

> GUEST'S VOICE
> Ye gawds, there's a gel out here with a
> poker!

She sees figures silhouetted in the light and we make out a worried older female face.

> MRS GAITER
> Isn't that . . . what are you doing?

Susan looks at the poker and then back at the woman.

> SUSAN
> Twyla said she's afraid of a monster in
> the cellar, Mrs Gaiter.

And then another face smoking a BIG CIGAR appears alongside MRS GAITER's.

                    MR GAITER
        And yer going to attack it with a
        poker, eh?

Cigar smoke wafts out from the room.

                    SUSAN
        Yes.

Mrs Gaiter raises her voice so the guests behind
can hear.

                    MRS GAITER
        Susan's our governess.

There is a change in the expression on the faces
peering out from the dining room to amused
respect.

                    GUEST
        She beats up monsters with a poker?

                    MR GAITER
        Actually, that's a very clever idea. Me
        daughter gets it into her head there's
        a monster in the cellar, you go in with
        a poker and make a few bashing noises
         while the child listens, and
          everything's all right.

                    MRS GAITER
        Is that what you're doing, Susan?

                    SUSAN
        Yes, Mrs Gaiter.

                    MR GAITER
        This I've got to watch, by Io! It's not
        every day you see monsters beaten up by
        a gel.

                    GUEST
        Absolutely.

There is a swish of silk and a cloud of cigar smoke as
the diners pour out into the hall.

INT. LORD DOWNEY'S STUDY - NIGHT

There is a knock at the door. He pushes his paperwork
aside and sits back.

                LORD DOWNEY
           Come in, Mister Teatime.

The door opens . . . but it's CARTER, one of the Guild's
servants, carefully balancing a tea tray.

                LORD DOWNEY
           Ah, Carter. Just put it on the table
           over there, will you?

                CARTER
           Yes, sir. I'm sorry, sir, I'll go and
           fetch another cup directly, sir.

                LORD DOWNEY
           What?

                CARTER
           Your visitor, sir.

                LORD DOWNEY
           What visitor? Oh, for when Mister
           Teati—

He stops. He turns.

There is a young man sitting on the hearthrug, playing
with the dog.

                LORD DOWNEY
           Mister Teatime!

                TEATIME
           It's pronounced Teh-ah-time-eh, sir.
           Everyone gets it wrong, sir.

                LORD DOWNEY
           How did you get in here?

                TEATIME
           Easily, sir. I got mildly scorched on
           the last few feet, of course.

Downey sees some lumps of soot on the hearthrug. And
then, with a 'how the hell did he do that?' look on his
face, glances at the fireplace.

                LORD DOWNEY
           The dog seems to like you.

TEATIME's face is fresh, open and friendly. It is
topped by curly hair. The face is actually quite

pretty, in a boyish sort of way . . . and hasn't stopped
smiling since it arrived. But then he turns from the
profile we've seen him in up to now and realise for the
first time that . . .

                    TEATIME
          I get on well with . . .

. . . he only has ONE EYE. The missing orb has been
replaced by a ball of glass.

                    TEATIME
          . . . animals, sir.

In close on Teatime's face we can see that the other
'good' eye has the smallest and sharpest pupil you have
ever seen - practically a pin-hole.

Downey nods and looks down at an open file on his desk.

                    LORD DOWNEY
          I have a report here that says that you
          nailed Sir George's dog to the ceiling.

                    TEATIME
          I couldn't have it barking while I was
          working, sir.

                    LORD DOWNEY
          Some people would have drugged it.

                    TEATIME
          Oh.

Teatime looks despondent for a moment, but then he
brightens.

                    TEATIME
          But I definitely fulfilled the
          contract. I checked Sir George's
          breathing with a mirror as instructed.

He pauses before reading on.

                    LORD DOWNEY
          Apparently his head was several feet
          from his body at that point.

Teatime appears to see nothing incongruous about this.

                    TEATIME
          (anxiously)

                    That was all right, wasn't
                    it, sir?

                         LORD DOWNEY
                    It . . . lacked elegance.

                         TEATIME
                    I thank you, sir. I am
                    always happy to be
                    corrected. I shall
                    remember that next time.

Downey takes a deep breath.

                         LORD DOWNEY
                    It is about the next
                    time that I wish to
                    talk.

He holds up the picture of the Hogfather
and looks at it.

                              LORD DOWNEY
                         As a matter of interest, how would you
                         go about inhuming . . .

Downey turns the picture so that Teatime can see it.

                              LORD DOWNEY
                         . . . this . . . gentleman?

Teatime leans forward, with a curious intent expression.

INT. GAITER'S HOUSE/HALL - NIGHT

TWYLA sits demurely at the top of the cellar stairs,
hugging her knees.

On the Guests' faces. Suddenly we hear a door opened
and shut. Then silence. Then a terrifying scream. One
woman faints and a Guest drops his cigar.

                         TWYLA
                    (calmly)
                    You don't have to worry. She always
                    wins.

There are thuds and clangs, and then a whirring noise,
and finally a sort of bubbling.

Susan pushes open the door. The poker thoroughly bent.

There is nervous applause.

                    MR GAITER
          Oh. Ha ha. Ver' well done. Ver'
          persykological. Clever idea, that,
          bendin' the poker. I expect you're not
          afraid any more, eh, my girl?

                    TWYLA
          No.

                    MR GAITER
          Ver' persykological.

                    TWYLA
          Susan says, 'don't get afraid, get
          angry'.

                    MRS GAITER
          Oh, thank you, Susan.

MRS GAITER is now a trembling bouquet of nerves.

                    MRS GAITER
          And, now, if you'd all like to come
          back into the parlour - I mean, the
          drawing room.

Susan watches the party as they make their way back up
the hall.

                    MR GAITER
          Dashed convincin', the way she bent the
          poker like that—

And the door shuts.

Susan waits.

                    SUSAN
          Have they all gone, Twyla?

                    TWYLA
          Yes, Susan.

                    SUSAN
          Good.

Susan goes back into the cellar.

Twyla waits until . . .

MONSTER FROM THE CELLAR

Oh, oh, mind the tail. Oh! oh!

. . . Susan emerges towing something large and hairy.
She hauls it up the steps by the tail . . .

INT. GAITER'S HOUSE/PASSAGE - NIGHT

. . . and down the other passage . . .

EXT. GAITER'S HOUSE/BACK YARD - NIGHT

. . . to the back yard, where she kicks it out.

                    MONSTER FROM THE CELLAR
        Ugghh.

                    SUSAN
        That's what we do to monsters.

Twyla watches carefully.

                    SUSAN
        Now it's back to bed for you, my girl.

INT. LORD DOWNEY'S STUDY - NIGHT

                    TEATIME
        Difficult, sir.

                    LORD DOWNEY
        Certainly.

                    TEATIME
        But I have devoted some time to it,
        sir.

Downey stops, and then looks shocked.

                    LORD DOWNEY
        You mean you've actually sat down and
        thought out how to inhume the
        Hogfather?

                    TEATIME
        Oh, yes, sir. And the Soul Cake Duck.
        And Death, sir.

Downey blinks again.

                    LORD DOWNEY
          They're imaginary creatures.

                    TEATIME
          Makes it a challenge.

Downey drums his fingers on the desk again.

                    TEATIME
          I suppose I just see things differently
          from other people.

Downey looks directly at Teatime.

                    LORD DOWNEY
          We may be able to see the complaint of
          Sir George's estate against you with
          regard to his dog rather differently . . .

Teatime's one good eye flickers with interest.

                    LORD DOWNEY
           . . . and approve your graduation to
          full membership of the Guild . . .

                    TEATIME
          'Take the dark', sir? Wear . . . black,
          sir?

                    LORD DOWNEY
           . . . if you agree to undertake this
          contract. With due elegance, of course.

                    TEATIME
          With elegance guaranteed, sir.

Teatime turns and starts to leave.

                    LORD DOWNEY
          Oh, Mister Teh-ah-time-eh.

Teatime stops.

                    LORD DOWNEY
          You . . . have . . . actually applied . . .
          yourself to a study of ways of killing
          Death?

                    TEATIME
          Only as a hobby, sir.

                    LORD DOWNEY
      But then, some people might say that he
      is technically immortal.

                    TEATIME
      Everyone has their weak point, sir.

Downey stares at him. Teatime smiles as he leaves.

INT. DEATH'S HOUSE/LIFETIMERS ROOM – NIGHT

The room is like a vast library with canyon-like rows
of shelves that go as high as you can see. It is dark.
Skulls decorate the ends of the cases.

Lining the shelves are rows of LIFETIMERS, like egg
timers made of wood and brass and glass. In DEATH's
house everything is in BLACK AND WHITE. (Only living
things are in colour in his domain.)

A few grains of sand fall in slow motion through the glass of one. Just as the last grains of sand fall, a SKELETAL HAND picks it up.

The Lifetimer slips into the depths of a dark CLOAK.

A SWORD HANDLE slots into a black scabbard.

 . . . and a blue glowing SCYTHE BLADE sweeps through the air.

INT. THE MENDED DRUM - NIGHT

Three men are sat round a table in a snug, lit by a candle stuck in a saucer. By their appearance and demeanour you would say they were criminals.

CHICKENWIRE, a scrawny man, is twisting a napkin between his hands like a garotte.

                    CHICKENWIRE
          's gone six. He's not coming. Let's go.

                    MEDIUM DAVE
          Sit down, will ya? Assassins are
          always fashionably late. 'Cos of
          style, right?

          MEDIUM DAVE is a solid-looking man with a
          thoughtful expression on his face.

                    CHICKENWIRE
          What's this? You never said
          anything about him being an
          Assassin.

                    MEDIUM DAVE
          It's Teatime. He's paying top
          rates. We can wait for top
          rates.

                    CHICKENWIRE
          Teatime? I've heard he's
          . . .

          He waves his hands vaguely,
          trying to find the right word.

                    CHICKENWIRE
          . . .mental. And he's
          got a funny eye.

34

There is a sound like distant thunder. It is Banjo
Lilywhite clearing his throat. He is an enormous man
for whom breathing is an intellectual exercise. He has
one blocked nostril and his mouth is open all the time,
as though he lives on invisible plankton.

                    BANJO
          What I don' unnerstan is. . .

A bottle is placed on the table in front of
Chickenwire. Chickenwire picks up the bottle and takes
care to keep it away from the candle flame.

                    BANJO
          . . .how longaz diz place had waiters?

There is a blur, and a knife shudders in the table
between Chickenwire's index and middle fingers.

He looks down at it in horror.

The 'waiter' puts down the tray and sits down.

The group stares at him in silence.

He gives them a friendly smile. He has a glass eye.
It's Teatime.

                    TEATIME
          Good evening.

Chickenwire tries to look straight at him
but quickly looks away.

                    TEATIME
          Do have another drink while we
          wait for the other members of
          our little troupe.

INT. GAITER'S HOUSE/SUSAN'S BEDROOM - NIGHT

Susan settles down with her
book once more.

Then . . .the door is pushed
open. It reveals the tousled
shape of Twyla, hanging onto
the doorknob with one hand.

TWYLA
Susan, there's a monster under my bed
again . . .

BOGEYMAN
Aagghh. Aagghh. Aagghh.

She sighs.

INT. GAITER'S HOUSE/TWYLA'S BEDROOM – NIGHT

TWYLA leaps into bed from a distance as a
precaution against claws.

There is a metallic tzing! as SUSAN withdraws
the bent poker from the little brass stand it
shares with the tongs and the coal shovel.

She leans over as if to tuck Twyla up. Then
her hand darts down and under the bed. She
grabs a handful of hair and pulls.

Before the bogeyman can get its balance, it's
spread-eagled against the wall with one arm
behind its back.

INT. THE MENDED DRUM – NIGHT

The entrance door opens slightly. A figure
comes in, but only just. It inserts itself
in the gap and sidles along the wall in a
manner calculated not to attract attention
. . . but of course it does.

The gang are looking over at him.

It looks at them over its turned-up
collar.

CHICKENWIRE
That's a wizard.

The figure hurries over and drags up a chair.
It's MR SIDENEY.

MR SIDENEY
(hissing)
No I'm not! I'm incognito!

36

MEDIUM DAVE
Yeah, right. You're just someone in a
pointy hat.

TEATIME
Mr Sideney here is indeed a wizard, a
student, anyway.

MEDIUM DAVE
This is my brother Banjo, this is
Chickenwire.

The wizard looks desperately at Teatime.

MR SIDENEY
I didn't want to come!

TEATIME
Mr Sideney's down on his luck
at the moment, hence his
willingness to join our little
venture.

CHICKENWIRE
So what's the job?

TEATIME
We don't do jobs. We
perform services. And
the service will earn
each of you ten
thousand dollars.

CHICKENWIRE
No one said anything
about there being magic
in all this.

MR SIDENEY
Well, I . . .

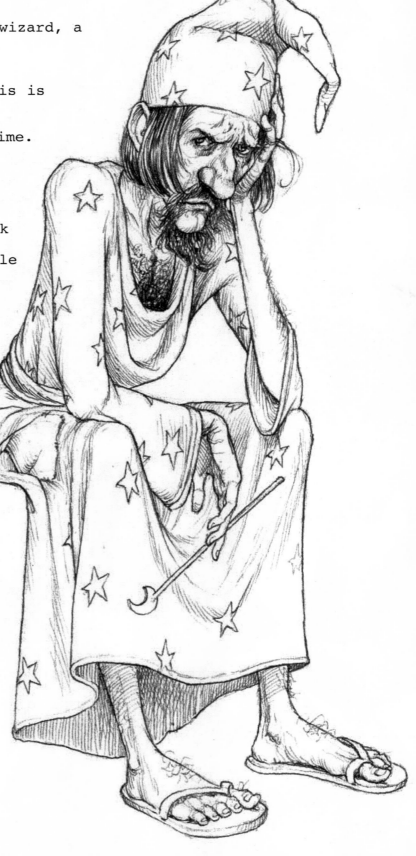

INT. GAITER'S HOUSE/TWYLA'S BEDROOM
- NIGHT

Twyla and GAWAIN bounce up and down
on their beds.

TWYLA
Do the Voice on it! Do the
Voice on it!

                    THE BOGEYMAN
No, not the Voice!

                    GAWAIN
Hit it on the head with the poker!

                    THE BOGEYMAN
Not the poker!

                    SUSAN
This is a friendly warning, understand?
Because it's Hogswatch.

                    THE BOGEYMAN
What are you, a witch or something?

                    SUSAN
I'm just . . . something. Now . . . you
won't be around here again, will you?
Or we'll put your head under the
blanket. It's got fluffy bunnies on it.

                    THE BOGEYMAN
Fluffy bunnies? No!

                    SUSAN
GO AWAY AND STOP BOTHERING ME.

The BOGEYMAN's POV of Susan's face as just for a moment
he sees a flash of BARED SKULL. He runs like hell.

                    BOGEYMAN

Aagghh!

                    TWYLA
That wasn't as much fun as the one last
month. You know, the one when you
kicked him in the trousers.

                    SUSAN
Just go to sleep now.

INT. THE MENDED DRUM - NIGHT

                    MEDIUM DAVE
     Locks?

Teatime looks at Medium Dave with tried patience all
over his face.

                    TEATIME
          We have a locksmith.

                    MEDIUM DAVE
          Who?

Teatime nods.

                    TEATIME
          Mr Brown.

                    MEDIUM DAVE
          Oh.

                    MR BROWN
          And you can help me carry this.

a bag of tools is heaved onto the table.

                    MR BROWN
          It's rather heavy.

MR BROWN, the wiry, bald, bespectacled man, takes
a seat.

Teatime turns and looks up at the bulk that is
Banjo.

                    TEATIME
          What is this?

                    MEDIUM DAVE
          This is my brother, Banjo.

Medium Dave rolls himself a cigarette.

                    TEATIME
          Does it do tricks?

Time stands still for a moment. The other men
look at Medium Dave.

The look on Medium Dave's face could kill.
His fingers apparently calmly tuck the
tobacco into a cigarette paper and raise
it to his lips.

                    MEDIUM DAVE
          No.

                    CHICKENWIRE
          He can lift up two men in each
          hand. By their necks.

                         BANJO
          Yur.

                        TEATIME
          Ha, ha, ha. He looks like a volcano.

                      MEDIUM DAVE
          Really?

And Medium Dave is up.

                      MEDIUM DAVE
          Wanna be fashionably late, do ya?

                        TEATIME
          I do so hope we're going to be friends,
          Mr Medium Dave. It really hurts to
          think I might not be among friends.

He gives him a bright smile. Then he turns back to the
rest of the table and looks Banjo up and down.

                        TEATIME
          Then I suppose we might as well make a
          start.

And he hits Banjo very hard in the mouth.

INT. YMPA/BANJO'S ROOM - NIGHT

Banjo is asleep. He snores in and, as he breathes out,
his lips flap open to reveal A GAP IN HIS FRONT TEETH.

The CAMERA tracks across his pillow and down to the
space between it and the sheet to reveal . . .

 . . . his TOOTH in big close-up.

Then a young female hand appears and picks up the tooth
from under his pillow.

                      VIOLET (O.C.)
            (whispering)
          Hello. My name's Violet, and I have
          been your Tooth Fairy for this evening.

Then in one deft movement she starts to put a SHINY
SILVER HALF-DOLLAR in the place of the Tooth. But
suddenly the coin drops from her fingers.

. . . a hand clamps over VIOLET BOTTLER's mouth. All we can see are her terrified eyes and her MOP OF RED HAIR as she drops out of shot.

Banjo's eyes open. He looks up.

EXT. STREET/ANKH-MORPORK - NIGHT

A CART trundles through the freezing foggy streets, the driver, ERNIE, hunched in his seat. He seems to be all big thick brown overcoat.

On the side of the cart in elegant sign writing is a picture of a wide child's grin with one tooth missing. Beneath it is written:

Tooth Fairy Bulk Collection: WORKING TOGETHER FOR A BRIGHTER SMILE.

A figure is suddenly on the box next to him.

The point of a KNIFE penetrates through four layers of thick clothing and stops just at the point where it pricks the flesh.

Ernie stops and stiffens abruptly.

>   ERNIE
> Er - yeah, there ain't nothing
> valuable, y'know, nothing valuable,
> only a few bags of t— t— t— t—

>   TEATIME
> Teeth, I know. My name's Teh-ah-time-
> eh. What is your name, sir?

>   ERNIE
> Ernie. Yes. Ernie.

Teatime turns his head slightly.

>   TEATIME
> Ha ha ha. Ha ha ha. Come
> along, gentlemen. This is my
> friend Ernie. He's going to
> be our driver for tonight.
> Put her in the back, Banjo.

Ernie sees the gang emerge from the fog and head for the cart. Banjo carries a long bundle over his shoulder. The bundle moves and makes

muffled noises. Sticking out of one end is
a mop of red hair.

> TEATIME
> Put her in the back, Banjo.

The group clamber into the cart. Ernie doesn't turn to
look at them.

Teatime withdraws the knife. Ernie stops holding his
breath and lets out an audible noise.

> ERNIE
> Mister, I ain't rightly allowed to carry
> passengers, ya know? Charlie'd give me a
> right telling-off—

> TEATIME
> Oh, don't you worry about that. We're
> all friends here!

Banjo can't take his eyes off Violet in the carpet.

> BANJO
> Our mam said 'no
> hittin' girls. Only
> bad boys do that',
> our mam said!

> MEDIUM DAVE
> Shut it.

> TEATIME
> Shssh! Ernie here
> doesn't wanna
> listen to our
> troubles.

Teatime does not take his
gaze off the driver as the
cart begins to clatter
across the cobbles.

> ERNIE
> W— w— where to,
> mister?

> TEATIME
> You know the way,
> Ernie. Behind the
> Unseen University.

> NARRATOR
> Where the students of magic are still
> hard at work on the night before
> Hogswatch.

EXT. UNSEEN UNIVERSITY/ROOF - NIGHT

The CAMERA tracks towards a small gable window. Just in
front of it a large TUBE emerges from the roof. It
begins to vibrate . . .

> PONDER STIBBONS (O.C.)
> It's just a shame we don't have any
> radiation shielding, Bursar.

INT. UNSEEN UNIVERSITY/HEX'S ROOM - NIGHT

 . . . PONDER STIBBONS, a young bespectacled student
wizard turns from the keyboard of HEX, a large Heath
Robinson THINKING ENGINE.

The University BURSAR is standing
nervously by.

> BURSAR
> You want radiation
> shielding, Mr Stibbons?

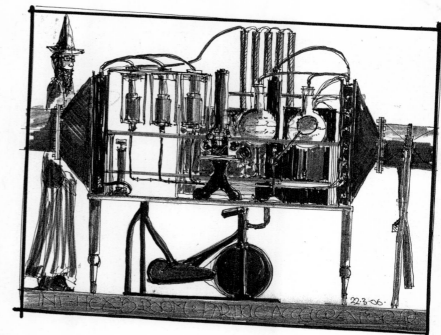

He is studying a blackboard with
a detailed drawing of what looks
like a chemistry set into which
a large metal tube runs and then
continues right around in a huge
loop.

> PONDER STIBBONS
> Advice from Hex,
> Bursar.

The Bursar looks at the
thinking engine.

> PONDER STIBBONS
> As the University won't supply us
> students with a thaumic particle
> accelerator, we're starting to build
> our own.

The Bursar looks at a group of student wizards gathered
around the beginnings of the accelerator. Sparks fly
around a beaker of volatile-looking liquid.

                    PONDER STIBBONS
          Safety first and all that.

The Bursar leaves the room in a hurry.

The accelerator sparks up.

Air pumps into its bellows and the big pipe starts to
vibrate dangerously.

STREET/ANKH-MORPORK - NIGHT

A cart is heading down a street towards the University.
A gable window flares with light

INT. UNSEEN UNIVERSITY/GREAT HALL - NIGHT

The Unseen University's Great Hall has been set for
the Hogswatchnight Feast. Tables are already
groaning under the weight of the cutlery. It is hard
to see where any food will fit among the drifts of
ornamental fruit bowls and forests of wine glasses.

The Bursar hurries in.

                         BURSAR
          Dean, have you seen the Head of
          Inadvisedly Applied Magic? I need some
          urgent advice.

The DEAN turns.

                         THE DEAN
          Ask the Chair of Indefinite Studies.

As the CHAIR OF INDEFINITE STUDIES looks round and
shrugs indefinitely, we hear a distant explosion.

The glasses and cutlery shake as if in a small
earthquake.

                CHAIR OF INDEFINITE STUDIES

          Um . . . Lecturer in Recent Runes.

                LECTURER IN RECENT RUNES

          Well, you see, it all depends.

Wizards stumble and the tables decorated for Hogswatch
Eve shake

MUSTRUM RIDCULLY, the
ARCHANCELLOR of the Unseen
University, wearing his dressing
gown and carrying a WASH BAG
enters the Hall. His voice
booms.

> RIDCULLY
> (to himself)
>> I don't know. In my day
>> when I was an
>> undergraduate I wouldn't
>> have been studying on
>> Hogswatchnight. It's just
>> not natural. I'd have
>> been sick twice by now . .
>> .

EXT. UNSEEN UNIVERSITY/ROOF – NIGHT

STUDENTS fight for space to retch out of the gable
window as the smoke billows round them.

STREET/ANKH–MORPORK – NIGHT

The cart turns a corner as the smoke above the
University disperses.

INT. UNSEEN UNIVERSITY/GREAT HALL – NIGHT

Ridcully turns his back from listening to the
distant sound of coughing and vomiting.

He turns back to the hall, which seems rather
empty. The wizards are all emerging from
beneath various tables.

> RIDCULLY
> Bursar . . . Bursar.

> BURSAR
> Hello, master.

> RIDCULLY
> The Dean . . . oh, there you are.

> BURSAR
> Archchancellor?

> RIDCULLY
> Members of the Faculty, I've decided,
> as a Hogswatch present to myself, to
> open up the late Archchancellor
> Weatherwax's old bathroom. Ha ha. So I
> don't have to sluice down with you
> fellows. I mean it's unhygienic. You
> can catch stuff.

The senior wizards of Unseen University look worried.

EXT. STREET/ANKH-MORPORK - NIGHT

The cart is heading towards the wall at the end of a
dead-end street. Half-collapsed houses, windows
smashed, doors stolen, lean against one
another on either side.

> ERNIE
> 'ere, I can't take you lot
> through the wall.

> TEATIME
> Listen, Ernie . . . Ern . . . you will
> take us through or, and I say this
> with very considerable regret, I
> will have to kill you.

> ERNIE
> But if'n I take you through—

> TEATIME
> What's the worst that can happen?
> You'll lose your job. Whereas if you
> don't, you'll die.

INT. UNSEEN UNIVERSITY/ ARCHCHANCELLOR'S BATHROOM - NIGHT

The wizards cross the snowy grounds to the bathroom.

> LECTURER IN RECENT RUNES
> Really, Mustrum, I think this is most
> unwise.

Ridcully flourishes his scrubbing brush.

> RIDCULLY
> Well, it said in the plans it was a
> bathroom. You chaps are all acting as if
> it was some kind of a torture chamber.

They stand and look at the door. Planks
have been nailed right across. A sign
hangs from the door reading DO NOT,
UNDER ANY CIRCUMSTANCES, OPEN THIS
DOOR.

                    THE DEAN
          A bathroom, designed by
          Bloody Stupid Johnson.

There is a pause. Even Ridcully has
to adjust his mind around this.

               LECTURER IN RECENT
                    RUNES
          Yeah, the late Bergholt
          Stuttley Johnson was the
          worst inventor in the
          world, Archchancellor.

                    RIDCULLY
          Yes, but not everything he
          made had a horribly fatal
          flaw. I mean think of that
          thing they use down in
          the kitchen for peelin'
          potatoes, for example.

               LECTURER IN RECENT
                    RUNES
          You mean that thing with the brass
          plate saying 'Improved Manicure
          Device'?

                    RIDCULLY
          Yeah, well, it's only water. Even old
          Johnson can't do much harm with water.

Maybe he has a point.

               LECTURER IN RECENT RUNES

          Ah, yes.

He gestures to MODO, the University's gardener and odd-
job DWARF, who stands by with a crowbar.

                    RIDCULLY
          Go to it, then.

The gardener salutes and raises the tool. There is the
sound of splintering wood.

EXT. STREET/ANKH-MORPORK - NIGHT

On a small tin, rather like a snuff-box. Ernie's hand opens it. There is glowing dust inside.

>   TEATIME
>   So . . .

>   ERNIE
>   Er . . . you just chucks it at the wall
>   there and it goes *twing*.

>   TEATIME
>   Really? May I try?

Teatime throws a pinch of dust into the air in front of the horse. It hovers for a moment and then produces a narrow, glittering arch in the air. It sparkles and goes . . .

    . . . *twing*.

>   BANJO
>   Aw, innat nice, eh, our Davey?

>   MEDIUM DAVE
>   Yeah.

>   TEATIME
>   And then you just drive forward?

>   ERNIE
>   Oh, yeah, right quick, mind, cos it
>   only stays open for a little while.

Teatime takes the little tin from his unresisting hand.

>   TEATIME
>   Thank you very much, Ernie. Very
>   much indeed.

There is a flash of a knife.

Ernie blinks, and then falls sideways off his seat.

>   TEATIME
>   Wasn't he dull?

Teatime picks up the reins and drives the cart towards the wall where . . . it passes through the soft place.

Snow begins to fall . . . on the recumbent shape of
Ernie.

It also falls through the materialising AUDITORS.

                    AUDITOR 1
          If he's supposed to be getting rid of
          the Hogfather, why is he going to the
          Tooth Fairy's Castle?

                    AUDITOR 2
          The tooth fairies are another childish
          belief.

                    AUDITOR 3
          Exactly.

                    AUDITOR 1
          Very elegant.

                    AUDITOR 4
          It is.

                    AUDITOR 2
          You have to start somewhere.

                    AUDITOR 3
          Once you have their little minds in
          your grip, it's goodbye Hogfather.

It stops. A dark shape is approaching through the snow.

                    AUDITOR 4
          It's him.

They fade hurriedly - not quite vanishing, but
spreading out and thinning until they are lost in the
background.

The dark figure is DEATH. From his skeletal face, blue-
illuminated eyes throw points of light in front of him.

He stops by Ernie and pulls a Lifetimer out of his
cloak. He looks at it and then at Ernie.

                    DEATH
          COULD I GIVE YOU A HAND?

Ernie looks up gratefully.

                    ERNIE
          Cor, yeah.

He gets to his feet, swaying a little.

                    ERNIE
          'Ere, your fingers ain't half
          cold, mister!

                    DEATH
          SORRY.

                    ERNIE
          What'd he wanna go and do that
          for? I did what he said. Coulda
          killed me.

Ernie feels inside his overcoat and pulls out
a small and, at this point, strangely
transparent silver flask.

                    DEATH
          YES.

                    ERNIE
          I always keep a nip on me these
          cold nights. Keeps me spirits up.

                    DEATH
          INDEED.

DEATH looks around briefly and sniffs the air.
He turns and catches a glimpse of the last
SPARKLES around the outline of the narrow
glittering ARCH in the wall as it fades to
nothing with a final *twing*.

                    ERNIE
          How'm I going to explain all this
          then, eh?

Ernie takes a pull from the flask.

                    DEATH
          SORRY? THAT WAS VERY RUDE OF ME. I
          WASN'T PAYING ATTENTION.

                    ERNIE
          I said, what'm I going to tell people?
          Letting some blokes ride off with my
          cart neat as you like . . . That's gonna
          be the sack for sure . . .

                    DEATH
          THERE AT LEAST I HAVE SOME GOOD NEWS,
          ERNEST.

Ernie listens and then looks at the corpse at his feet.

                         DEATH
          AND, THEN AGAIN, I ALSO HAVE SOME BAD
          NEWS.

Ernie looks back up at the seven-
foot skeleton with a scythe.

                    ERNIE
          So . . . I'm dead, then.

                    DEATH
          CORRECT.

It sinks in for Ernie.

                    ERNIE
          Aaggh.

                    DEATH
          NOW TELL ME ABOUT THESE
          BLOKES WHO STOLE YOUR CART
          AND KILLED YOU.

Ernie disappears. And after a moment
DEATH vanishes as well, leaving the
street empty, except for the fleshy
abode of the late Ernie.

The grey shapes come back into
focus.

                    AUDITOR 2
          Honestly, Death gets worse and worse.

                    AUDITOR 1
          He seems to like humans.

                    AUDITOR 3
          So illogical. But the beauty of the
          Assassin's plan is that he can't
          interfere.

                    AUDITOR 4
          But Death can go everywhere.

                    AUDITOR 1
          No. Not quite everywhere.

And, with ineffable smugness, the Auditors turn and
look towards the wall where the cart has passed
through.

The CAMERA TRACKS slowly towards and then 'through' the wall into WHITE . . .

INT. TOOTH FAIRY'S CASTLE/FOOT OF TOWER - DAY

The CAMERA emerges from white to reveal . . .

. . . the peaceful and quiet vast central entrance hall. The walls are white marble and stone. Long sweeping stairs wind their way up the central tower, which seems to go on forever.

Teatime, Medium Dave, Mister Brown, Chickenwire, Mister Sideney and Banjo carrying Violet in the carpet enter and look around . . . and two Tooth Guards look back . . .

Chickenwire has pounced on one's back and, moving like lightning, has tightened a wire around the guard's neck as we discover where his name comes from. The other is dispatched by Medium Dave.

There is a dull thud as the guards slump to the floor and vanish.

EXT. ROOF TOPS/ANKH-MORPORK - NIGHT

As far as we can see are the snow-capped rooftops of Ankh-Morpork. In the foreground we see what appears to be a body falling and hitting one of the roofs.

INT. DEATH'S HOUSE/LIFETIMERS ROOM - NIGHT

DEATH picks up a LIFETIMER. The last few grains of sand are running out. He puts it inside his robes and is about to move away when he sees that the one next to it on the same shelf is also expiring.

He picks that one up too. Then he sees that there are several in this area all about to run out. He stops, straightens. Something's happening and it's not quite right.

INT. TOOTH FAIRY'S CASTLE/FOOT OF TOWER - DAY

Two lightly armed guards wearing TOOTH-SHAPED HELMETS are patrolling the castle.

                        TOOTH GUARD 1
                  Great job but you look a right tit
                  wearing these helmets.

Just as the other guard nods Banjo grabs them by the
scruff of their necks and lifts them off the ground.

Their legs struggle as they adjust their helmets just
in time for Banjo to bang their heads together and they
collapse in a heap on the floor.

EXT. ROOF TOPS/ANKH-MORPORK - NIGHT

 . . . another body falls from the sky . . .

INT. TOOTH FAIRY'S CASTLE/FOOT OF TOWER - DAY

Chickenwire has his arms around another guard. Medium Dave
spits on his fist and punches the guard in the kidneys.

The guard's pale face is frozen in a rictus of pain.
Then he crumples into a heap of limbs that rolls down
the steps until it reaches the bottom and is still.
Slowly it evaporates . . .

EXT. ROOF TOPS/ANKH-MORPORK - NIGHT

 . . . and another . . . and another . . .

INT. TOOTH FAIRY'S CASTLE/FOOT OF TOWER - DAY

Looking on, Teatime smiles.

INT. DEATH'S HOUSE/LIFETIMERS ROOM - NIGHT

From an adjacent room there is a surge in the sound of
falling sand, and Death collects more Lifetimers.

INT. TOOTH FAIRY'S CASTLE/FOOT OF TOWER - DAY

A Tooth Guard runs up the stairs . . . straight into
Teatime.

                        TEATIME
             Hello. My name's Teatime. What's yours?

INT. DEATH'S HOUSE/LIFETIMERS ROOM - NIGHT

DEATH looks round . . .

. . . as ALBERT, DEATH's 67-year-old small, hunched
assistant, also roused by the sound, puts his head
around the door. He is carrying a FRYING PAN with BACON
and EGGS in it. Albert too looks towards the adjacent
room, worried.

> DEATH
> ALBERT, SOMETHING IS NOT RIGHT.

Albert shrugs his shoulders.

> RAVEN (O.C.)
> Ah, too right.

Albert and DEATH turn to see that the RAVEN is looking
behind them . . . They look to where he is looking.

One of the shelves of Lifetimers swings open like a
door to reveal the adjacent room . . .

INT. DEATH'S HOUSE/LIFETIMERS SECRET ROOM - NIGHT

DEATH walks into the secret room. It's smaller than the
main Lifetimers room (merely the size of a cathedral!)
and DEATH looks at another row of Lifetimers.

But these are . . . different . . . these look as though
they are made of highlights and shadows with no real
substance at all. They have labels on them. The larger
ones have the names of the gods on them. The smaller
ones . . .

A bony hand runs along the labels: The Tooth Fairy -
The Sandman - John Barleycorn - The Soul Cake Duck . . .
and then THE HOGFATHER.

DEATH leans towards it and looks more closely at the
Hogfather Lifetimer. The SAND is running so fast we can
see the level dropping. When he looks up, he appears,
if a skull can be otherwise, even more mortified . . .

> ALBERT
> This is the mythological person's room.
> How can one of them die?

> DEATH
> SOUL CAKE DUCK. THE TOOTH FAIRY. THE
> HOGFATHER. OH DEAR.

Behind him . . .

                    ALBERT
          Oh dear, oh dear. ha ha.

Death turns to his assistant.

                    DEATH
          ALBERT. WE MAY NOT HAVE MUCH TIME.

INT. GAITER'S HOUSE/SCHOOL ROOM – NIGHT

The city's clocks strike six
in the distance.

Susan is tidying up the
schoolroom and getting things
ready for the morning. She
picks up the things the
children have left lying on
the floor and looks around
the room.

There are two stockings
hanging from the mantelpiece
of the small schoolroom grate
. . .

 . . . Twyla's paintings, all
blobby blue skies, violently
green grass and red houses
with four square windows . . .

She straightens up and
stares at them, her
fingernails beating a
thoughtful tattoo on a
wooden pencil case.

The CAMERA tracks in to TWYLA's PAINTING . . . towards
one of the child-like houses and right into the doorway
. . .

                    VOICE FROM PICTURE

          Hello. Can you hear me? Help! Hello?
          Hello? Please, somebody help. Please
          somebody do something!

as we . . .

                                        DISSOLVE TO:

57

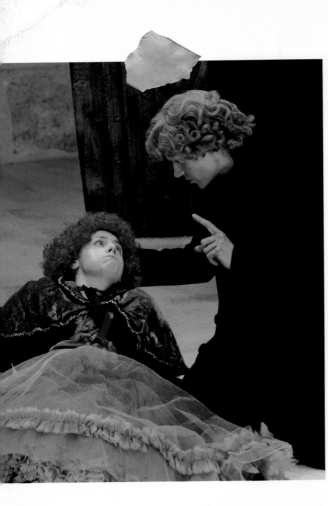

INT. TOOTH FAIRY'S CASTLE/FOOT OF TOWER – DAY

Banjo gently lays the roll of carpet on the floor. He steps back. As he does Teatime nods to Medium Dave who steps forward, takes hold of one end of the roll and pulls hard.

The roll unravels and Violet Bottler is unfurled across the white stone. She rolls to a stop looking rather pale.

> VIOLET
> Help me, somebody please help
> me. Somebody, please help me!
> Uh, I don't know what you're
> expecting me to say but—

A hand clamps over her mouth. Teatime is crouched by her.

> TEATIME
> Sshhh. Questions first, babble later.

Teatime pulls her head up by the mop of red hair.

> TEATIME
> Now, Miss Bottler. I'd like you to
> think of me as a friend . . .

INT. GAITER'S HOUSE/SCHOOL ROOM – NIGHT

On Susan. She is looking at Twyla's painting. It is as if she has watched something terrible.

INT. UNSEEN UNIVERSITY/ ARCHCHANCELLOR'S BATHROOM – NIGHT

Mustrum Ridcully is sat in a chair wearing a dressing gown.

> RIDCULLY
> How are we doing Mr Modo?

Modo salutes.

> MODO
>
> Tanks are filled and I've stoked the
> boilers, Mr Archchancellor, sir.

Ridcully gets up and walks down the corridor.

THE DEAN
You did read the sign on that door,
Ridcully?

Ridcully ignores him.

BURSAR
Yes.

RIDCULLY
You mean the sign which said 'do not
under any circumstances open this
door'?

THE DEAN
Yes.

BURSAR
That's right, yes.

THE DEAN
Surely it was sealed up for a reason?

RIDCULLY
Oh, they only wrote that to keep people
out.

BURSAR
Yes, that's right, that's what people
do.

THE DEAN
But don't say I didn't warn you.

RIDCULLY
By Jeeve, that's the ticket.

MODO
I still haven't worked out where all
the pipes lead.

RIDCULLY
(Happily)
Oh, we'll find out. Ha ha. Don't you
fear! Ha ha!

The room is a sanitary poem in mahogany, rosewood and
copper. Every pipe and brass tap has been polished
until they gleam.

Ridcully removes his hat and puts on a shower cap of
his own design. In deference to his profession, it's
pointy. He summons a yellow rubber duck.

> RIDCULLY
> Man the pumps, Mr Modo. Or dwarf 'em,
> of course, in your case. Ha ha!

> BURSAR
> Oh. Oh. Aagghh.

Modo hauls on a lever. The pipes start a hammering
noise and steam leaks out of a few joints.

The rest of the wizards back away.

Ridcully shuts the frosted door of the Ablutorium
behind him, his face beaming with expectation.

INT. TOOTH FAIRY'S CASTLE/DISPLAY CASE
ROOM 1 - DAY

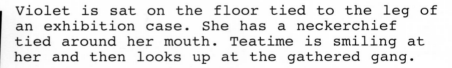

Violet is sat on the floor tied to the leg of
an exhibition case. She has a neckerchief
tied around her mouth. Teatime is smiling at
her and then looks up at the gathered gang.

Behind him range long lines of museum-like
exhibition cabinets. He leads the gang down
the aisle. Chickenwire looks into one of the
cases. It is packed full of teeth.

> TEATIME
> She's a tooth fairy, but she's not *the*
> tooth fairy. Sshh.

> CHICKENWIRE
> Teeth?

> TEATIME
> What d'you expect in the Tooth Fairy's
> castle?

> CHICKENWIRE
> Gives me the creeps just thinking about
> it.

> TEATIME
> You don't have to think. You just have
> to do what I say.

> MEDIUM DAVE
> All of 'em?

TEATIME

Every last one.

MEDIUM DAVE

Put 'em in a pile.

CHICKENWIRE

But that's millions.

TEATIME

Mr Brown, I want you to unlock every
door you can find.

Mr Brown nods grumpily and heads off.

Medium Dave goes over to Teatime confidentially.

MEDIUM DAVE

What's this really all about?

Teatime gestures to Banjo, who is stood by himself
staring at a case, and steps close to Medium Dave's
face.

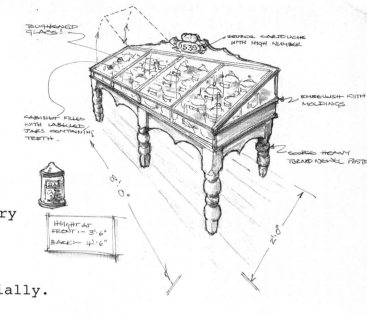

TEATIME
Does he believe in things like the Soul
Cake Duck? The Sandman? The Tooth
Fairy?

MEDIUM DAVE
Yeah. Even the Hogfather.

TEATIME
Cos after we're finished here, not even
he will.

And with that Teatime turns. With one lightning
movement he plunges his knife into the glass of one of
the cases.

With a sickening crunch tiny teeth begin to trickle
onto the floor.

EXT. THE CASTLE OF BONES - NIGHT

DEATH rides a large white horse, BINKY, across the sky.

DEATH
ONWARDS, BINKY, TO THE HOGFATHER'S
CASTLE OF BONES.

Binky skims the tops of the fir trees as the icy
landscape beneath him rises into a snow-covered
mountain range.

As the horse climbs we begin to see the outline of a
snow-covered structure that seems to be almost sculpted
out of the mountain side.

The pillars at the entrance are hundreds of feet high.
Each of the steps leading up is taller than a man. They
are the grey-green of old ice. Ice. Not bone. There are
faintly familiar shapes to the pillars, possibly a
suggestion of femur or skull, but it is made of ice:
THE HOGFATHER'S CASTLE OF BONES.

Binky flies down towards it. As we get closer we can
see that there is something inside the entrance to the
castle. In front of it, a blur of pink moves towards
the forest . . .

INT. THE CASTLE OF BONES/ENTRANCE - NIGHT

Binky doesn't quite fly up the high stairs, more walks
on a ground level of his own devising, into the
building. Beneath the columns is the HOGFATHER'S
SLEIGH, with HOGS, snuffling the snow in front of it.

There is a slash of oxblood-red colour draped across
the seat.

A sound behind him makes DEATH turn. The PIXIE HELPER
(from scene 2 with the Hogfather) is staggering out
from inside the Castle of Bones, DRUNK and dishevelled.
He takes a swig from one of two SHERRY GLASSES.

> PIXIE HELPER
> First Hogswatch off in a thousand
> years. Ooh. Even if I'm going to have
> the mother of all hangovers in the
> mornin—

Then he sees DEATH and stops in his tracks. He looks at
the glasses, then back up to DEATH and then runs like
hell.

DEATH watches him go and then turns back to the sleigh.

INT. TOOTH FAIRY'S CASTLE/DISPLAY CASE ROOM 1 - DAY

Chickenwire smashes cases while Medium Dave forces
others open to load the teeth into sacks. In the
foreground a handful of teeth cascades onto the floor.

INT. GAITER'S HOUSE/TWYLA'S BEDROOM - NIGHT

Susan is sat on the bed in mid-debate with the
children.

> GAWAIN
> And how can the Hogfather bring all the
> presents to everyone all at the same
> time?

> TWYLA
> Unless there are lots of Hogfathers . . .

> SUSAN
> Look, you've always believed in the
> Hogfather, yes?

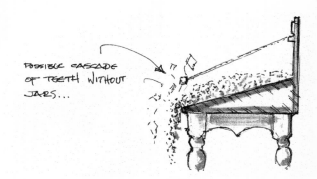

POSSIBLE CASCADE
OF TEETH WITHOUT
JARS...

                    TWYLA
        Yes.

                    SUSAN
        Well, if you don't believe in him he
        won't come down the chimney.

Gawain looks unconvinced.

                    TWYLA
        It's a very small chimney.

                    SUSAN
        And a very small stocking if you don't
        go to sleep.

EXT. THE CASTLE OF BONES - NIGHT

On inspection, Death sees that the red is the
HOGFATHER'S COSTUME on the Hogfather's sleigh but there
is no Hogfather.

INT. GAITER'S HOUSE/TWYLA'S BEDROOM - NIGHT

As Susan tucks Twyla in there is a flicker of concern
across her face. What HAS got into them?

EXT. THE CASTLE OF BONES - NIGHT

Death lowers the Hogfather's costume and looks
into the distance.

INT. VIRGINIA PROOD'S HOUSE/BEDROOM - NIGHT

We pass a pile of Hogswatch presents, food and
decorations . . . and then a mousetrap baited with
a piece of pork crackling. A MOUSE peeks its nose
out of a hole in a skirting board. It scurries
along the wall and out of sight. There is the
snap of a mousetrap. The mouse now lies beneath
it.

Then its head turns to the BLACK-CLAD FIGURE that
has appeared by the wainscoting. DEATH OF RATS
passes his scythe over the mouse, and with that,
the mouse leaves its still body in the trap.

The Death of Rats looks around the room with
interest.

It is brightly decorated. Ivy and
mistletoe hang in bunches from the
bookshelves. Brightly coloured
streamers festoon the walls.

The Death of Rats leaps onto the
table and into a glass of SHERRY,
which tips over and breaks. A puddle
spreads around four TURNIPS and
begins to soak into a note which has
been written rather awkwardly on pink
writing paper.

Dere Hogfather,

*For Hogswatch I would like a drum an a dolly an a
teddybear an a Gharstley Omnian Inquisision Torchure
Chamber with Wind-up Rack and Nearly Real Blud
You Can Use Again. I have been good. I hop the
Chimney is big enough but my friend Willaim Says you
are my father really.*

Yrs. Virginia Prood

The Death of Rats nibbles a bit of the pork pie left
out for the Hogfather.

A few lumps of soot thump into the grate. The scraping
becomes louder, is followed by a moment of silence and
then a clang as something lands in the ashes and knocks
over a set of ornamental fire-irons.

The Death of Rats jumps down from the table onto a bare
branch of oak that stands in a pot by the table and
watches carefully as a RED-ROBED FIGURE pulls itself
upright and staggers across the hearthrug, rubbing its
shin where it has been caught by the toasting fork.

It reaches the table and reads the note. There is a
groan.

The turnips and the pork pie are pocketed.

The figure scans the dripping note for a moment, and
then turns around and approaches the mantelpiece.

A red-gloved hand takes down a stocking. There is some
creaking and rustling and it is replaced, looking a lot
fatter - the larger box sticking out of the top has,
just visible, the words:

The figure stands back and pulls a list out of its pocket. It holds it up to the hood and appears to be consulting it. The hood hides all the face of the figure in red, apart from a long white beard. It waves its other hand vaguely at the fireplace, the sooty footprints, the empty sherry glass and the stocking. Then it bends forward, as if reading some tiny print.

> VOICE
> AH, YES . . . ER . . . HO. HO. HO.

With that, it ducks down and enters the chimney.

INT. ARCHCHANCELLOR'S BATHROOM - NIGHT

Ridcully's voice booms out through the thick clouds of steam until . . . the song rises to a falsetto and stops abruptly. All Modo can hear is a ferocious gushing noise.

Modo spins a wheel. The gushing sound gradually subsides. Moments later he pushes open the door and helps a rather pale Ridcully out and onto a bench.

> RIDCULLY
> (high-pitched voice)
> Ooh . . . Ooh . . . this tap is marked
> 'Old Faithful' . . .

Ridcully coughs.

> RIDCULLY
> (low normal voice)
> . . . which I think perhaps we might
> leave alone for now.

> BURSAR
> This is . . . a most peculiar Hogswatch.

EXT. VIRGINIA PROOD'S HOUSE/ROOF - NIGHT

There is a sleigh hovering above the rooftops.

> VOICE BEHIND SACKS
> Any mustard? They're a treat with
> mustard.

The red-hooded figure turns back. It is DEATH dressed as the Hogfather.

DEATH picks up the reins.

> DEATH
> APPLE! SAUCE!

The pigs' legs blur. Silver light flicks across them, and explodes outwards. They dwindle to a dot, and vanish. The sleigh is gone.

The Grim Squeaker climbs out of the chimney in time to watch him go.

> DEATH OF RATS
> SQUEAK? SQUEAK SQUEAK SQUEAK!

SUBTITLE: Strictly speaking, that's not part of the job description.

EXT. SKY - NIGHT

The sleigh soars onwards through time and space. DEATH looks over his shoulder at the sacks.

They all appear to have sticking out of the top a teddy bear, a toy soldier, a drum and a red-and-white candy cane.

> DEATH
> I'M FINDING THE BEARD A BIT OF A TRIAL.

> VOICE BEHIND SACKS
> Well, at least it's keeping you in the right frame of mind, master. In character, that sort of thing.

> DEATH
> BUT GOING DOWN THE CHIMNEY? WHERE'S THE SENSE IN THAT?

A head thrusts itself out from the pile. It appears to belong to the oldest, most unpleasant pixie in the universe. The fact that it is underneath a jolly little green hat with a bell on it does nothing to improve matters. It is ALBERT . . . in an ill-fitting Pixie costume.

ALBERT
It's gotta be chimbleys, innit, eh? A
bit like the beard, really.

He waves a crabbed hand containing a thick wad of
letters, many of them on pastel-coloured paper.

ALBERT
D'you think these little buggers'd be
writing to someone who can walk through
walls if they knew? Oh, and that
reminds me, the 'Ho, ho, ho' could do
with some more work, if you don't mind
my saying so.

DEATH
HO. HO. HO.

ALBERT
No, no, no! No! You gotta
put a bit more life in it,
sir, er, no offence
intended. You've gotta do a
big fat laugh sir. You
know, like 'Ho! Ho! Ho!'
You gotta sound like you're
pissing brandy and you're
crapping plum pudding,
sir, if you'll pardon my
Klatchian.

Albert pulls out a packet of
CIGARETTE PAPERS and starts to make
a roll-up.

DEATH
REALLY? HOW DO YOU KNOW
ALL THIS?

ALBERT
Well, I used to be
young myself once,
sir, surprising as it
may seem.

Albert opens a pink sack. It
seems to be nearly all horses.
Most of them are grinning.
Just as he reaches for his
TOBACCO POUCH in his coat, the
wind blows the paper away.

INT. TOOTH FAIRY'S CASTLE/FOOT OF TOWER – DAY

Chickenwire empties a sack of teeth into the beginnings
of a pile. He sidles towards Medium Dave.

> CHICKENWIRE
> These teeth give me the creeps.

> MEDIUM DAVE
> Just keep going.

> CHICKENWIRE
> But why are we piling them all up?

> MEDIUM DAVE
> You don't wanna know. Quicker all the
> teeth are in the pile, quicker we're
> out of here with our money. No one ever
> laid a punch on Banjo since our mam
> died.

> CHICKENWIRE
> Tough but fair, your Ma. Ah, I recall
> that time she strangled Glossy Ron with
> his own leg.

> MEDIUM DAVE
> Yeah.

Chickenwire sweeps some stray teeth into the pile.

> CHICKENWIRE
> Maybe the both of us could creep up on
> him and, er . . .

> MEDIUM DAVE
> (sarcastically)
> Yeah.

Chickenwire realises that this was probably not a good
idea.

> CHICKENWIRE
> I keep thinking about that glass eye
> watching me. I keep thinking that he
> can see right in my head.

> MEDIUM DAVE
> Don't worry, he doesn't know what
> you're thinking.

> CHICKENWIRE
> Yeah, well, how do you know?

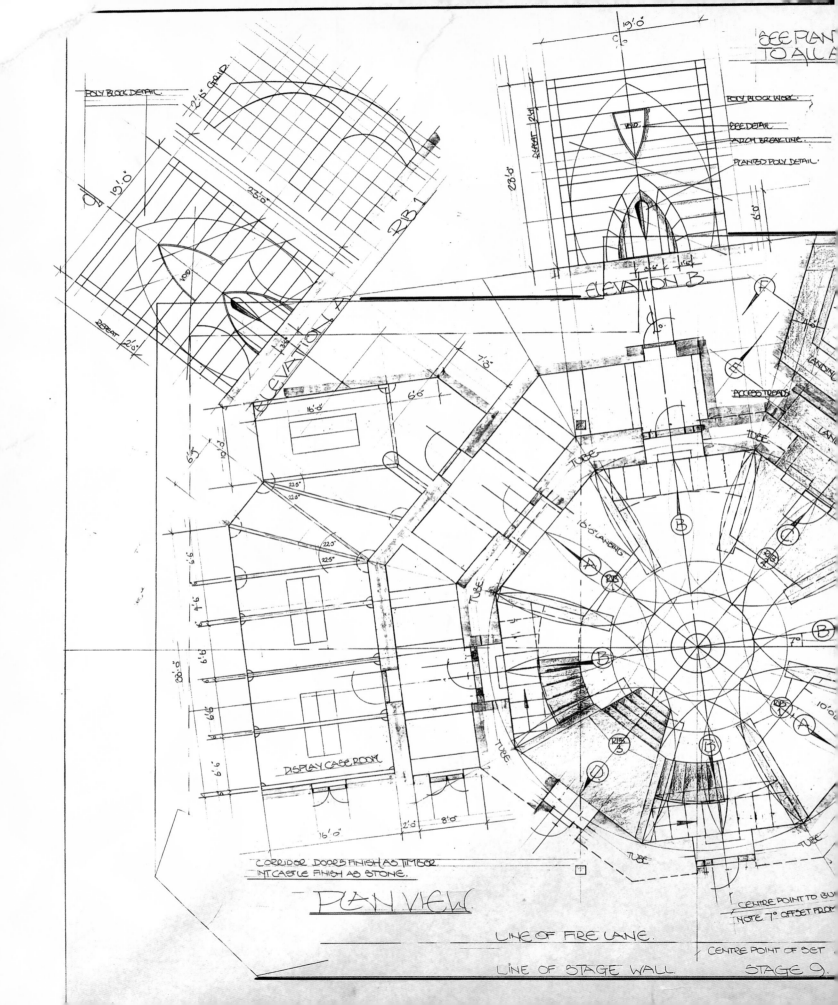

POLY BLOCK DETAIL.

19'0"

23'0"

RB1

REPEAT 2'0"

6'5"

10'0"

88'0"

6'9"

6'9"

6'9"

6'9"

16'0"

2'0"   8'0"

CORRIDOR DOORS FINISH AS TIMBER.
INT CASTLE FINISH AS STONE.

PLAN VIEW.

LINE OF FIRE LANE.

LINE OF STAGE WALL.

19'0"

POLY BLOCK WORK.
SEE DETAIL.
ARCH BREAK LINE.
PLANTED POLY DETAIL.

ELEVATION B

7'3"

6'6"

16'0"

22.5°
22.5°

22.5°
22.5°

DISPLAY CASE ROOM

LANDING

ACCESS TREADS

TUBE

TUBE

16'0" LANDING

A
RB1
B

B

TUBE

TUBE

TUBE

RB1
A

RB1
B

0

CENTRE POINT TO BU
NOTE 7° OFFSET FROM

CENTRE POINT OF SET

STAGE 9.

SEE PLAN
TO ALL A

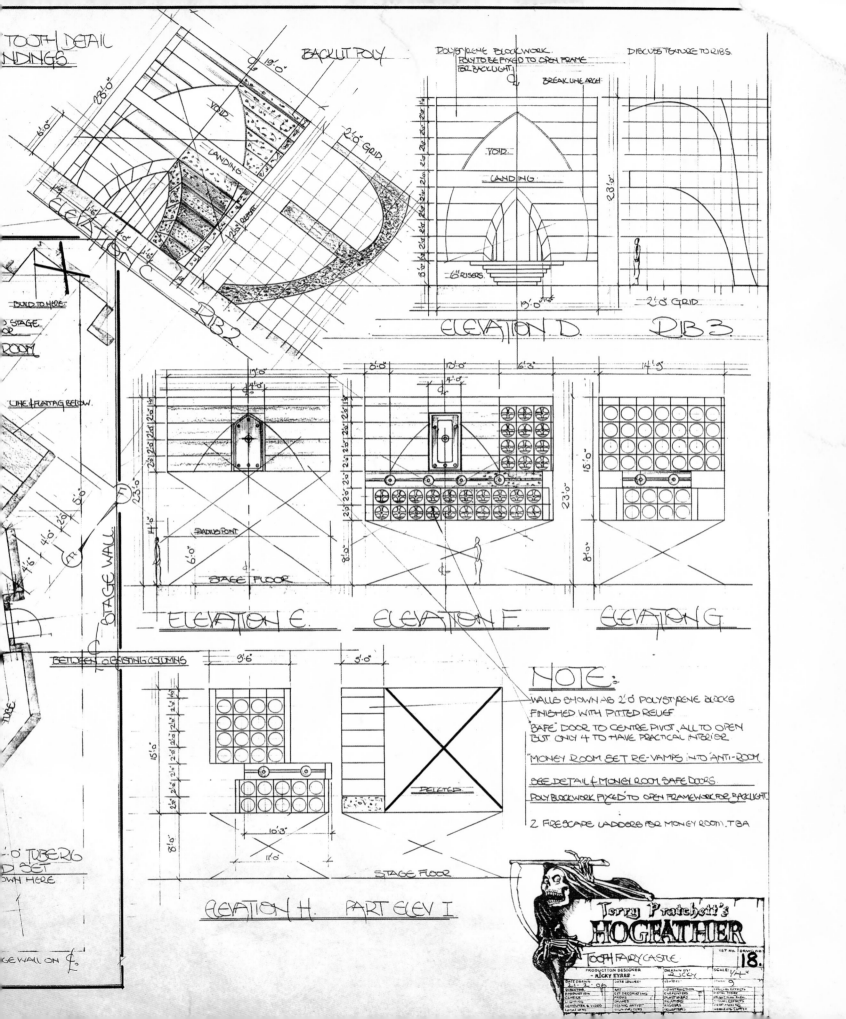

                         MEDIUM DAVE
                  You're still alive.

INT. GAITER'S HOUSE/SCHOOL ROOM - NIGHT

Susan enters the schoolroom. Inside, something has
changed . . .

Susan glares at the stockings, but they are still
unfilled.

She looks across to the window which is half open . . .

She hears a clicking noise behind her and then a voice
comes from the shelves on the other side of the room.

                         RAVEN (O.C.)
                  These damn eyeballs are hard, aren't
                  they?

                         SUSAN
                  They're walnuts, not eyeballs.

                         RAVEN
                  Aagghh!

The walnuts bounce around her on the floor.

Susan turns, races across the room. The
Raven flies off the shelf and out of
the window. Susan slams it shut behind
him.

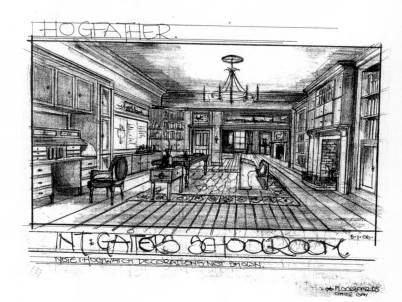

                    SUSAN
         I don't want you back in my
         life, understand?

The Raven taps at the window pane.

But the muffled sound draws Susan
closer to listen for a moment.

                    RAVEN

         Don't say you haven't been
         warned.

                    SUSAN
         Warned?

EXT. JAMES RIDDLE'S ROOF – NIGHT

The pigs and sleigh are on the roof. DEATH steps out of
the chimney. Albert is waiting in the sleigh.

                    ALBERT
         Ah, did you check the list?

Albert gives a last lick to a ROLL-UP and puts it in
his mouth. He starts to look for a light.

                    DEATH
         COULDN'T REALLY MAKE HEAD NOR TAIL OF
         IT, TO TELL YOU THE TRUTH. I DON'T
         NORMALLY CARE IF THEY'VE BEEN NAUGHTY
         OR NICE.

DEATH gives Albert a pork pie which he carefully
examines.

                    ALBERT
         Ha ha.

                    DEATH
         I CAN FEEL BELIEF IN THE HOGFATHER
         FADING.

                    ALBERT
         What's that?

DEATH
IT LOOKS VERY BAD.

ALBERT
Nah, 's just where
something's been nibbling
it, that's all.

Albert licks his fingers and bites
into the pork pie.

DEATH
I MEAN THE SITUATION. I
FEAR WE MAY BE TOO LATE.

ALBERT
(with mouth full)
Oh well. Never say die,
master, that's our motto.

DEATH
I CAN'T SAY IT'S EVER
REALLY BEEN MINE.

And with that DEATH tugs on the reins and the sleigh
flies away.

INT. GAITER'S HOUSE/SCHOOL ROOM - NIGHT

Susan is still for a moment. She looks over to the
ticking clock. The PENDULUM STOPS MOVING and FREEZES
mid-swing.

Then, suddenly . . .

. . . there is a scrabbling sound far overhead.

A few flakes of soot drop down the chimney.

There is a tapping on the window again. Susan turns.

RAVEN
You'd better watch out.

And with a flutter of wings he is gone.

INT. TOOTH FAIRY'S CASTLE/FOOT OF TOWER - DAY

Teatime is with Sideney by the start of a pile of
teeth.

74

Brainse Bhaile Thormod
Ballyfermot Library

Tel. 6269324/5

                    TEATIME
        . . . Because if the Hogfather still
        comes to town as a result of a magical
        misjudgment on your part then you will
        no longer be my friend, Mr Sideney.

The wizard is holding a piece of chalk.

                    MR SIDENEY
        I understand, sir.

                    TEATIME
        Do you have a lot of friends,
        Mr Sideney?

                    MR SIDENEY
        Um . . . quite a few, actually.

                    TEATIME
        (apologetically)
        I don't have many. Don't seem to
        have the knack. On the other hand
        . . . I don't seem to have any
        enemies at all.

                    MR SIDENEY
        (shaking)
        It's a . . . very enemy-friendly
        spell, sir.

Teatime stares right into Mr Sideney's
face.

                    MR SIDENEY
        That is . . . very simple. And
        will make the pile of teeth
        very—

His discomfort is only broken when we
hear a voice shouting from high up in
the tower.

                    CHICKENWIRE (O.C.)
        Mr Teh-a-time-eh.

Teatime looks up.

At the release of tension in Sideney's fingers he
snaps the chalk.

                    MR SIDENEY
        —dangerous.

INT. GAITER'S HOUSE/SCHOOL ROOM - NIGHT

DEATH is stood in the middle of the nursery carpet. The pillow under Death's red robe slips gently down.

> SUSAN
>
> Grandfather . . . !

She walks around him.

> SUSAN
>
> This is Hogswatch! It's supposed to be jolly, with mistletoe and holly, and— and other things ending in olly! It's a time when people are meant to feel good about things and eat until they explode! A time when they want to see all their relatives . . .

She stops mid-sentence.

> SUSAN
>
> I mean it's a time when humans are really human, and they don't want a . . . a skeleton at the feast! Especially one, I might add, who's wearing a false beard and has got a damned cushion shoved up his robe! I mean, why?

Susan pulls the pillow out from under his cloak.

DEATH looks nervous.

> DEATH
>
> ALBERT SAID IT WOULD HELP ME GET INTO THE SPIRIT OF THE THING.

Susan looks over at the sounds of struggling from the chimney.

> ALBERT
>
> Ow . . . ow.

Susan turns back to DEATH. He is tucking his artificial Hogfather stomach back in.

> SUSAN
>
> This is a real job. And I was looking forward to a real Hogswatch, where normal things happen with normal people in a normal house! And suddenly the old circus comes to town. Well, I don't

know what's going on, but you can just
leave, right now!

There is a muffled curse, a rush of soot, and Albert
lands in the grate.

>   ALBERT
> Ow. Aagghh. Oh. Oh.

>   SUSAN
> Albert . . .

>   ALBERT
> Buggr'it! Aaggh. Master, I'm stuck.

                         SUSAN
         . . . the pixie?! Oh, come along in,
         do. If the real Hogfather doesn't turn
         up soon there's not going to be enough
         room for him.

                         DEATH
         HE WON'T BE JOINING US.

                         SUSAN
         So what have you turned up for? And if
         it's for business reasons, I will add,
         then that outfit is in extremely poor
         taste . . .

     The pillow slides softly onto the rug.

                         DEATH
         THE HOGFATHER IS . . . UNAVAILABLE.

                    SUSAN
At Hogswatch?

                    DEATH
YES.

                    SUSAN
Why?

                    DEATH
HE IS . . . LET ME SEE . . . THERE ISN'T
AN ENTIRELY APPROPRIATE HUMAN WORD, SO
. . . LET'S SETTLE FOR . . . GONE. YES. HE
IS GONE.

DEATH looks down at Susan with a pained expression.

Susan is pacing in front of him.

                    SUSAN
How can the Hogfather be gone? He's . . .
isn't he what you are? Anth . . .

                    DEATH

ANTHROPOMORPHIC PERSONIFICATION. YES.
HE HAS BECOME THE SPIRIT OF HOGSWATCH.

                    SUSAN
    (ignoring him)
And while he's gone you've taken over?
That's sick!

Albert brushes past her and opens the door. Susan
pushes it shut quickly.

DEATH leans down. Susan stares up into the blue glow of
his eyes.

A couple of letters appear in DEATH's hand.

                    DEATH
I SEE THE GIRL WRITES IN GREEN CRAYON
ON PINK PAPER WITH A MOUSE IN THE
CORNER. THE MOUSE IS WEARING A DRESS.

                    SUSAN
I ought to point out that she decided
to do that so that the Hogfather would
think she was sweet. Including the
deliberate bad spelling. But look, why
are you doing the . . .

                    DEATH
        SHE SAYS SHE IS FIVE YEARS OLD.

                    SUSAN
        Seven. In cynicism, she's about thirty-
        five. But why are you doing the . . . ?

                    DEATH
        BUT SHE BELIEVES IN THE HOGFATHER?

                    SUSAN
        She'd believe in anything if there was
        a dolly in it for her. But you're not
        going to leave without telling me . . .

DEATH hangs the stockings back on the mantelpiece.

                    ALBERT
                 (belches)

        Susan turns to Albert who has helped
        himself to the glass of sherry and couple
        of turnips that the children have left on
        the table.

                    SUSAN
        And what are you doing here,
        Albert? I thought you'd die if you
        ever came back to the world!

                    DEATH
        AH, BUT WE ARE NOT IN THE WORLD.
        WE ARE IN THE SPECIAL CONGRUENT
        REALITY CREATED FOR THE HOGFATHER.
        NORMAL RULES HAVE TO BE SUSPENDED.
        HOW ELSE COULD ANYONE GET AROUND
        THE ENTIRE WORLD IN ONE NIGHT?

                    ALBERT
                 (leering)
        's right. I'm one of the
        Hogfather's Little Helpers, me.
        It's official. I've got the
        little pointy green hat with a
        bell and everything.

Albert spits into the fireplace.

                    ALBERT
        'ave you been good? Have ya?

Susan stares at him.

                        80

                    DEATH
          NOW WE MUST BE GOING. HAPPY HOGSWATCH.
          AND, UM . . . OH, YES:

Susan is about to speak again.

                    DEATH
          HO. HO. HO.

Albert wipes his mouth.

                    ALBERT
          Ha ha. It's a nice drop of sherry, this.

Rage overtakes Susan's curiosity.

                    SUSAN
          You've actually been drinking the
          actual drink little children leave out
          for the actual Hogfather?

                    ALBERT
          Well, yeah, why not? He won't be drinking
          any more, will he, eh? Ha ha, not where
          he's gone.

                    SUSAN
          And how many have you had, may I ask?

                    ALBERT
            (Happily)
          Hmm? Well, dunno, haven't been counting.

                    DEATH
          ONE MILLION, EIGHT HUNDRED THOUSAND,
          SEVEN HUNDRED AND SIX. AND SIXTY-EIGHT
          THOUSAND, THREE HUNDRED AND NINETEEN
          PORK PIES. AND ONE TURNIP.

                    ALBERT
          Oh, yeah, well, it looked pork-pie-
          shaped. But then everything does, after a
          while, doesn't it?

                    SUSAN
            (screaming)
          Why are you doing this?

                    DEATH
          I AM SORRY. I CANNOT TELL YOU. FORGET
          YOU SAW ME. IT'S NOT YOUR BUSINESS.

                    SUSAN
          Not my business? How can you say—

                              DEATH
          YOU WANTED TO BE NORMAL. GOOD NIGHT
          . . . GRANDDAUGHTER . . .

                              ALBERT
          Sleep tight.

                              ALBERT
          I know I shall.
            (hiccoughs)
          Pardon.

The clock strikes, twice, for the half-hour. It is
still half past six but the PENDULUM starts swinging
again.

And they are gone.

INT. TOOTH FAIRY'S CASTLE/STAIRCASE - DAY

Teatime strides up the stairs to find Mr Brown picking
a lock. The last tumbler turns and he steps back.

                              MR BROWN
            (grumpy)
          There are a lot of doors. I hope this
          is the one.

Teatime sniffs the air, then slowly turns the handle
and enters the room silently.

INT. TOOTH FAIRY'S CASTLE/DISPLAY CASE ROOM 2 - DAY

Teatime takes one step into doorway and stops. He
surveys the room and looks disappointed.

                              TEATIME
          This isn't the room we're looking for.
          Just teeth in here. Keep going, Mr
          Brown.

Then in a flash he turns behind the door.

                              TEATIME
          Boo!

The guard cowering behind it jumps out of his skin.
Terror spreads across his face.

                              GUARD
          Aagghh.

INT. TOOTH FAIRY'S CASTLE/FOOT OF TOWER - DAY

The dead guard falls, SMASH, directly into the
CAMERA . . .

EXT. ROOFTOPS/ANKH-MORPORK - NIGHT

. . . and lands on the roof of the Unseen University
where his hat drops off onto the window ledge below

INT. CHILD'S BEDROOM/ANKH-MORPORK - NIGHT

DEATH fills a stocking. Albert preps a roll-up.

>   ALBERT
> Susan'll try to find out what this is
> all about, you know.

>   DEATH
> OH DEAR.

>   ALBERT
> Especially after you told her not to.

>   DEATH
> YOU THINK SO?

>   ALBERT
> Oh yeah.

Albert carefully rolls up his cigarette.

>   DEATH
> DEAR ME. I STILL HAVE A LOT TO LEARN
> ABOUT HUMANS, DON'T I?

>   ALBERT
> Oh . . . I dunno . . .

>   DEATH
> OBVIOUSLY IT WOULD BE QUITE WRONG TO
> INVOLVE A HUMAN IN ALL THIS. THAT IS
> WHY, YOU WILL RECALL, I CLEARLY FORBADE
> HER TO TAKE AN INTEREST.

>   ALBERT
> Yep . . . yes you did . . .

>   DEATH
> BESIDES, IT'S AGAINST THE RULES.

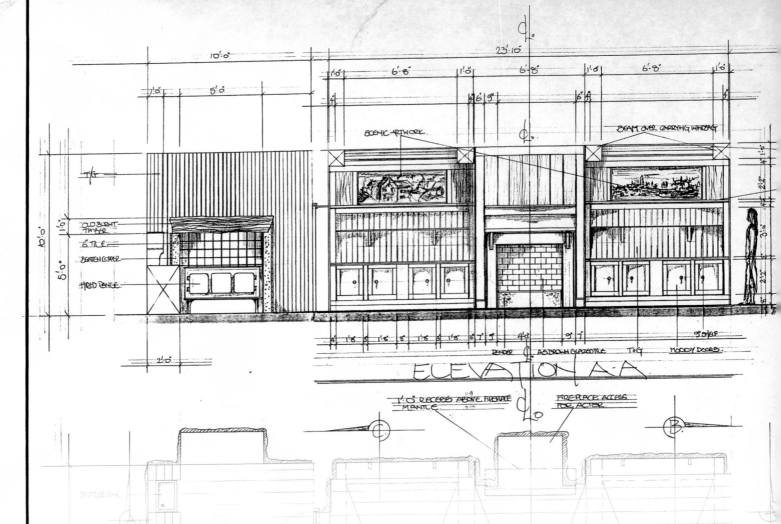

ELEVATION A-A

ALBERT
Yeah, well, of course that's a shame
really, because she likes to break 'em,
don't she?

DEATH
YOU MIGHT THINK I'VE ALREADY THOUGHT OF
THAT, BUT I COULDN'T POSSIBLY COMMENT.

DEATH stares ahead for a moment and then shrugs.

DEATH
AND WE HAVE MUCH TO DO. WE HAVE THE
HOGFATHER'S PROMISES TO KEEP.

Albert bends down to seal his cigarette and the draft
blows his tobacco up the chimney.

ALBERT
Right.

INT. GAITER'S HOUSE/SCHOOL ROOM - NIGHT

Susan stands by the fireplace looking at
the dolly in Twyla's stocking, thinking.

> SUSAN
> Has he done something to the real
> Hogfather?

She looks out into the middle distance,
thinking.

INT. GAITER'S HOUSE/TWYLA'S BEDROOM - NIGHT

Susan quietly opens the door to the
bedroom.

Twyla and Gawain are sound asleep.

Susan watches them for a moment and then
goes over and kisses them gently.

She stands up. From the back of her head
the HAIR starts to MORPH from its prim
governess style into freaky GOTH MODE
until we reveal a look of steely resolve
on Susan's face.

She shuts her eyes and CLICKS her fingers. When they
open she hears the clock stop ticking. The last tick is
long-drawn-out, like a death rattle.

Time stops. But duration continues.

And she is gone.

INT. GAITER'S HOUSE/BACK STAIRS - NIGHT

Susan hurries down the stairs and lets herself out of
the front door.

EXT. GAITER'S HOUSE - NIGHT

Snow hangs motionless in the air. It sparkles
electronically as she walks through it.

There is traffic in the street, but it is fossilised in Time. The flakes gather on her coat, leaving behind her a Susan-shaped tunnel in the hanging snow.

She reaches the gate to the house where the snow mounds the bushes and trees in pure white.

There is no noise. The curtains of snow shut out the city lights.

EXT. GAITER'S HOUSE/SIDE - NIGHT

A white horse is waiting for her

> SUSAN
>
> Binky.

Then suddenly there are hoof-beats and the floating snow bursts open and Binky is there. He trots round in a circle, and then stands and steams. Susan looks at him, deciding, for the briefest of moments . . . and then jumps on his back.

Binky and Susan fly off . . .

And as the snow starts to fall again, the Auditors materialise. The snow falls through them as they ruminate.

> AUDITOR 3
> Can she be eliminated?

> AUDITOR 2
> Oh yes, she's mostly human.

> AUDITOR 3
> Oh good.

> AUDITOR 4
> Then can we go back to just
> concentrating on running the universe?
> Making sure that gravity works and that
> atoms spin?

> AUDITOR 1
> Yes, when there's not an atom of belief
> left in the world.

> AUDITOR 3
> And the Hogfather is just the
> beginning.

EXT. ARCHCHANCELLOR'S BATHROOM - NIGHT

Ridcully slowly and carefully dries his feet on a big fluffy towel. He leans closer to inspect between his toes.

>   THE DEAN
>   What are you looking for, Mustrum?
>
>   RIDCULLY
>   Ha ha. My father always said 'when you
>   see a lot of people bathing together,
>   the Verruca Gnome is running around
>   with his little sack'.

He shouts into the Ablutorium.

>   RIDCULLY
>   Ha ha. Modo! Any sign of the
>   Verruca Gnome down there, old
>   boy? Ha ha.

EXT. UNSEEN UNIVERSITY/ROOF - NIGHT

...and someone lands abruptly in the thick snow and rolls down the pitch of the roof.

EXT. UNSEEN UNIVERSITY/COURTYARD - NIGHT

At the bottom of a drainpipe it shoots out into a snowdrift.

Moments later it struggles out of the snow. It wears a stained black suit and, on its head a 'bowler' or 'derby' HAT. The hat is pressed down very firmly so that as the creature has long pointy ears, these are forced out sideways and give it the look of a small malignant wing-nut. Over its shoulder it has a small CLOTH SACK.

The gnome-like thing goes back to the bottom of the drainpipe. Without pausing, he starts to climb up the inside of the pipe.

EXT. DEATH'S HOUSE – NIGHT

DEATH's extensive lawn stretches out in front of the house, surrounded by extensive areas of topiary. In the foreground is an ornamental fish pond surrounded by cheerful little skeletal fishing gnomes.

INT. DEATH'S HOUSE/LIBRARY – NIGHT

DEATH's desk is a mess. Books lie open, piled on one another. There is a note in his non-serifed handwriting. It looks as though he's been trying to work something out:

MEMO: DON'T FORGET THE SOOTY FOOTPRINTS. MORE PRACTISE ON THE HO HO HO. CUSHION.

> RAVEN
> Welcome home, Susan. You took your
> time.

Susan turns.

> SUSAN
> I don't do family reunions.

Susan looks through the papers, glancing up but quickly ignoring a FRAMED PICTURE of herself as a child on DEATH's knee.

By the desk stands DEATH's SWORD. Its thin blue blade pulses.

INT. DEATH'S HOUSE/LIFETIMERS ROOM – NIGHT

Susan looks round briefly at the infinite shelves of Lifetimers and is about to leave when she notices an open door. She goes over to it.

It is disguised. A whole section of shelving, complete with its whispering glasses, has slid out.

She steps into the doorway and starts down the spiral staircase.

INT. DEATH'S HOUSE/LIEFETIMERS SECRET ROOM – NIGHT

The secret smaller room on the other side is lined
floor to ceiling with more hourglasses that Susan can
just see dimly in the light from the big room. She
steps inside . . .

We have seen these hourglasses before. These are the
ones made of highlights and shadows with no real
substance we saw when DEATH was in this room . . . the
Lifetimers of the Gods, and beneath them, smaller
ones . . .

> SUSAN
> The Sandman? Soul Cake Duck? Tooth
> Fairy? The Hogfather.

Susan stops.

Something crunches under SUSAN's feet.

There are shards of glass on the floor. She reaches
down and picks up the biggest. Only a few letters
remain of the name etched into the glass. HOGFA

> SUSAN
> Grandfather . . . what have you
> done?

Susan leaves the room and as she does, in the
darkness, among the spilled sand, there is a faint
sizzle and a tiny spark of light . . .

EXT. ROOF TOP – NIGHT

DEATH throws the sack into the back of the sleigh,
climbs in after it and hitches his belt.

> DEATH
> THIS CUSHION IS STILL UNCOMFORTABLE.

> ALBERT
> You're doing well, master. Soot in
> the fireplaces, footprints, swigged
> sherries, the sleigh tracks all over
> the roofs . . . No, no, it's got to
> work.

> DEATH
> YOU THINK SO?

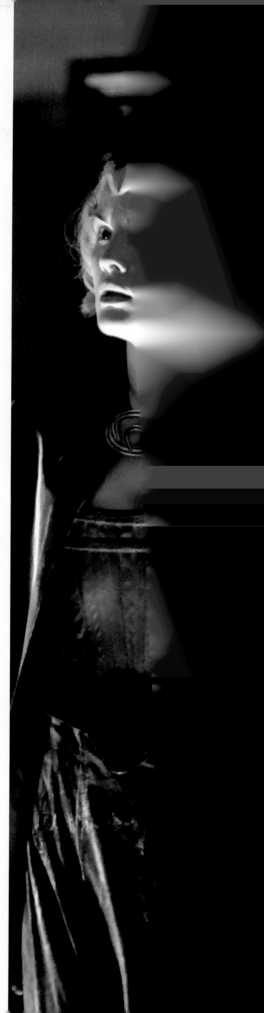

ALBERT
Oh, yeah. Oh, here's a little tip, though. 'Ho. Ho. Ho.' will do. Don't say, 'Cower, brief mortals', ha ha.

DEATH looks down dejectedly to see the hundreds of snowy roofs without sleigh tracks ahead of them.

DEATH
OH REALLY? MMM. SO MANY CHIMNEYS. IT WOULD BE SO MUCH QUICKER IF I LOST THE CUSHION.

ALBERT
Yeah, well, I mean if we're going to give Susan enough time to succeed, the little perishers need to believe in you, master . . . no, I mean the Hogfather. So you've got to look the part, master.

Albert looks down at his notebook to see the endless list of names.

ALBERT
I tell you, what'd be really good to boost belief is a public appearance.

DEATH
OH. I DON'T NORMALLY DO THEM.

ALBERT
Yeah, but the Hogfather's more've a public figure, master. I tell you what, one good public appearance would do more good than any amount of letting the kids see you by accident.

DEATH
REALLY?

ALBERT
And I know just the place.

INT. CRUMLEY'S DEPARTMENT STORE – NIGHT

A magnificent GROTTO takes up nearly all of the first floor of the store. The Hogfather's SLEIGH is a work of art in itself. It has delicate silver curly bits on it, every twinkling star carefully glued on. The PIGS look really real and a wonderful shade of pink.

VERNON CRUMLEY, the store owner, looks proudly on.

And the kiddies are queuing up with their parents and watching the display owlishly.

Vernon looks across to the middle of the floor.

There is a cashier in a little cage. Staff are taking money from customers, putting it in a little clockwork cable car, and sending it whizzing overhead to the cashier, who makes change and starts it rattling back again.

>   SHOPPER
>   Thank you very much indeed.

>   VERNON CRUMLEY
>   Everything's ticketyboo on the floor?

>   CASHIER
>   Yes Mr Crumley.

>   VERNON CRUMLEY
>   Jolly good.

EXT. ROOF TOP – NIGHT

DEATH thinks for a moment.

>   DEATH
>   LET'S GO SLEIGH THEM.

And then he pauses.

>   DEATH
>   I DON'T KNOW IF YOU NOTICED, ALBERT,
>   BUT THAT WAS A PUNE, OR PLAY ON WORDS.

ALBERT
     Ho, Ho, Ho, sir.

Albert flourishes his completed roll-up.

INT. CRUMLEY'S DEPARTMENT STORE - NIGHT

Mr Crumley tucks his fingers in the pockets of his
waistcoat and beams. Then he looks down at the pile of
coins in front of the cashier.

Suddenly . . . a bright little zig-zag crackles off them
and earths itself on the metal grille.

Mr Crumley turns to look at the Hogfather display as
it . . .

 . . . changes . . . or rather, disintegrates and shatters.
The four pink papier-mâché pigs explode.

A cardboard snout bounces off Mr Crumley's head.

The sleigh has changed. The splendour of it is lying in
glittering shards around a sleigh that looks as though
it has been built of crudely sawn tree trunks laid on
two massive wooden runners. It looks ancient and there
are faces carved on the wood, nasty crude grinning
faces that look quite out of place.

And there, sweating and grunting in the place where the
little piggies had been, were . . . well, they look like
pigs. They are huge, grey and bristly and have pointy
ears and rings through their noses, more like
 . . . HOGS. A cloud of acrid mist hangs over each one.

One of the pigs turns to look at Crumley with small,
red eyes.

                    HOG
     Ghnaaarrrwnnkh?

               VERNON CRUMLEY
     Ooohhh.

INT. CRUMLEY'S DEPARTMENT STORE/KIDS DEPT - NIGHT

Parents are yelling and trying to pull their children
away from the Hogfather's sleigh, but they aren't
having much luck. The children are gravitating towards
it like flies to jam.

Mr Crumley runs towards the terrible thing, waving his hands.

                    VERNON CRUMLEY
          Stop it! Stop it! You're frightening
          the little kiddies!

But behind him . . .

                    SMALL BOY (O.C.)
          Wow! They've got tusks! Cool!

And then we see his sister also glued to the display.

                    SMALL BOY'S SISTER
          Hey, look, that one's doing a wee!

A tremendous cloud of yellow steam arises from behind the boar.

Mr Crumley, tears of anger streaming down his face, fights through the milling crowd until he reaches the Hogfather's Grotto. He grabs a frightened PIXIE.

                    VERNON CRUMLEY
            (shouting)
          It's the Campaign for Equal Heights
          that've done this, isn't it! They're
          out to ruin me!

The pixie hesitates.

A red and white figure pushes its way through the crush and rams a false beard into Mr Crumley's hands.

                    GROTTO HOGFATHER
          That's it. I don't mind the smell of
          the oranges and the damp trousers but I
          ain't putting up with this.

He stamps off through the queue.

                    GROTTO HOGFATHER (O.C.)
          And he's not even doin' it right!

                    VERNON CRUMLEY
          What?

Mr Crumley forces his way onward.

95

INT. CRUMLEY'S DEPARTMENT STORE/GROTTO – NIGHT

SOMEONE is sitting in the big chair. There is a child on his knee.

Crumley looks concerned and confused.

From Crumley's POV we see that it is definitely in something like a Hogfather costume, but his eye keeps slipping and won't focus. The figure is on the very edge of his vision.

> VERNON CRUMLEY
> What's going on here? Eh? Come on.

A hand takes his shoulder firmly. He turns round and looks into the face of a GROTTO PIXIE. It looks as though its costume has been put on somewhat askew and in a hurry.

> VERNON CRUMLEY
> Ah. Who are you?

The pixie puts a cigarette in its mouth and leers at him.

> ALBERT
> You can call me Uncle Heavy.

> VERNON CRUMLEY
> You're not a pixie!

> ALBERT
> No, I'm a fairy cobbler, mister. Now just shh, keep quiet.

Behind Crumley . . .

> DEATH (O.C.)
> AND WHAT DO YOU WANT FOR HOGSWATCH, SMALL HUMAN?

Mr Crumley turns in horror.

INT. DEATH'S HOUSE/LIBRARY - NIGHT

There is a flutter of wings behind Susan as she searches along the shelves in the canyons of DEATH's huge library.

Susan stops.

There are several shelves, not just one book on the Hogfather. The first volume seems to be written on a book made of animal skin.

> RAVEN
> The autobiographies write down everything that happens to you as it happens . . .

> SUSAN
> I know. I used to live here, remember?

She looks more closely at the book.

> SUSAN
> But I can't read this! The letters are all . . . odd . . .

> RAVEN
> Oh, so I suppose now you'll be wanting my words of occult wisdom . . .

Susan pauses and then reluctantly nods.

> RAVEN
> Ethereal runes. The Hogfather ain't human, after all.

Susan looks up.

> RAVEN
> 'n I suppose a bit of warm liver's out of the question . . . ?

INT. ARCHCHANCELLOR'S BATHROOM - NIGHT

The Archchancellor is dressed in a robe, cutting his toenails. The clippings fall into an envelope.

> RIDCULLY
> (singing again)
> On the second day of Hogswatch I . . . sent my true love back . . . a nasty little letter. Mmm, ha ha, and a

partridge in a pear tree . . .

Ridcully suddenly spins. A corner of wet towel catches
a small creature on the ear and flicks it onto its
back. It's the GNOME in THE BOWLER HAT with the little
sack.

                    RIDCULLY
          What's your game, man? Small-time
          thief, are you?

The gnome slides backwards on the soapy surface.

                    VERRUCA GNOME
          You ain't supposed to be able to see
          me!

                    RIDCULLY
          Well I'm a wizard! We can see things
          that are really there, you know. What's
          in this bag?

Ridcully looks interested, and starts to undo the
string.

                    VERRUCA GNOME
              (pleading)
          You'll really wish you hadn't, mister!

                    RIDCULLY
          Oh will I? What're you doing here,
          young man?

The gnome gives up.

                    VERRUCA GNOME
          Well you know the Tooth Fairy? Well,
          it's sort of like the same business . . .

                    RIDCULLY
          You mean you take things away?

                    VERRUCA GNOME
          Er, not take away, as such. More sort
          of . . . bring . . .

                    RIDCULLY
          Ah . . . bright new teeth?

                    VERRUCA GNOME
          Er . . . like new verrucas.

>   RIDCULLY
> Ugghh, ugghh, oh. You're him!

Archchancellor Ridcully nods, looks at the sack,
tightens it back up and then thinks again.

INT. CRUMLEY'S DEPARTMENT STORE/GROTTO – NIGHT

In front of the usurping HOGFATHER is a small CHILD of
indeterminate sex who seems to be mostly woollen bobble
hat.

>   BOBBLE HAT CHILD
> (sniggering)
> I saw your piggie do a wee!

>   DEATH
> OH . . . UM . . . GOOD.

>   BOBBLE HAT CHILD
> It had a gwate big—

>   DEATH
> (hurriedly)
> WHAT DO YOU WANT FOR HOGSWATCH?

> BOBBLE HAT CHILD'S MOTHER
> She wants a . . .

The HOGFATHER snaps his fingers
impatiently. The MOTHER's mouth slams
shut.

The child seems to sense that this is a
once-in-a-lifetime opportunity . . .

>   BOBBLE HAT CHILD
> I wanta narmy. Anna big castle wif an
> active dwarbridge and a swored.

Albert nudges the HOGFATHER.

>   ALBERT
> I think they're supposed to say thank
> you, master.

>   DEATH
> ARE YOU SURE? PEOPLE DON'T, NORMALLY.

>   ALBERT
> No, I meant to the Hogfather, which is
> you, right?

As Albert is just about to light his cigarette, DEATH
glares at him and nods his head towards the child.
Albert hides the fag behind his back.

                    ALBERT
          Sorry.

                    DEATH
          YES, OF COURSE. AHM. YOU'RE SUPPOSED TO
          SAY THANK YOU.

                    BOBBLE HAT CHILD
          'nk you.

                    DEATH
          AND BE GOOD. THIS IS PART OF THE
          ARRANGEMENT.

                    BOBBLE HAT CHILD
          'es.

                    DEATH
          THEN WE HAVE A CONTRACT.

INT. UNSEEN UNIVERSITY/ARCHCHANCELLOR'S BATHROOM – NIGHT

Ridcully lifts the lid of an ornate jar marked BATH SALTS and pulls out a bottle of wine.

>   RIDCULLY
>   Ah, ah, verrucas, eh?

>   VERRUCA GNOME
>   Wish I knew why.

He extracts the cork with a pop.

>   RIDCULLY
>   You mean you don't know?

>   VERRUCA GNOME
>   Nope. Suddenly I wake up and I'm the
>   Verruca Gnome.

>   RIDCULLY
>   Well that's strange . . .

Ridcully frowns, then shakes his head and points to a pot supported on the wall by decorative mermaids.

>   RIDCULLY
>   Anyway, amazing bathroom, ain't it?
>   It's even got a special pot for your
>   toenail clippings.

>   VERRUCA GNOME
>   Special pot for your toenail clippings?

>   RIDCULLY
>   Well, you can't be too careful. Get
>   hold of something like somebody's nail
>   clippings, hair, teeth, you've got 'em
>   under your control. I mean that's real
>   old magic.

He takes a swig of wine, thinking hard, and empties the envelope of his new clippings into the circular pot . . .

>   DISSOLVE TO:

INT. TOOTH FAIRY'S CASTLE/FOOT OF TOWER – DAY

. . . the circular pile of teeth from above now towers over the gang.

Banjo sweeps the very last tooth into the pile.

Teatime, on the stairs high above, smiles.

>   TEATIME
> Children of the world . . .
> prepare to think as you
> are told.

He gestures to Sideney.

>   TEATIME
> Mr Sideney. Your big no
> misjudgments, magic moment.

Sideney pulls the small piece of chalk from behind his ear and takes a big breath.

The tiny stub of chalk in Sideney's fingers draws a chalk line. It comes to a stop as it reaches the end of another chalk line.

INT. CRUMLEY'S DEPARTMENT STORE/GROTTO – NIGHT

The HOGFATHER reaches into his sack and produces . . . a very large model CASTLE with pointy blue cone roofs on turrets suitable for princesses to be locked in . . . a box of several hundred assorted KNIGHTS and . . . a SWORD. It is four feet long and glints along the blade.

The mother takes a deep breath.

>   BOBBLE HAT CHILD'S MOTHER
>   (screaming)
> You can't give her that! It's not safe!

>   DEATH
> IT'S A SWORD. THEY'RE NOT MEANT TO BE
> SAFE.

>   VERNON CRUMLEY
>   (shouting)
> But she's a child!

>   DEATH
> IT'S EDUCATIONAL.

                    VERNON CRUMLEY
              What if she cuts herself?

                    DEATH
              THAT WILL BE AN IMPORTANT
              LESSON.

Albert whispers urgently.

                    DEATH
              REALLY? OH, WELL. IT'S NOT FOR ME TO
              ARGUE, I SUPPOSE.

The blade turns wooden.

                    BOBBLE HAT CHILD'S MOTHER
              And she doesn't want all that
              other stuff! She's a girl! And
              anyway, I can't afford big posh
              stuff like that!

                    DEATH
                 (bewildered)
              I THOUGHT I GAVE IT AWAY.

              BOBBLE HAT CHILD'S MOTHER
              You do?

                    VERNON CRUMLEY
                 (horrified)
              You do? You don't! That's our
              merchandise! You don't just give it
              away! Hogswatch isn't about giving
              everything away!

He sees that people were watching and . . .

                    VERNON CRUMLEY
              I mean . . . yes, you do give things
              away, but you have to buy them first.

                    BOBBLE HAT CHILD'S MOTHER
              You mean this is all free?

Mr Crumley looks helplessly at the toys. Then he tries
to look hard at the new HOGFATHER.

Crumley's POV tells him that this is a fat jolly man in
a red and white suit . . . or does it?

                    VERNON CRUMLEY
              It . . . would seem to be . . .

INT. UNSEEN UNIVERSITY/HEX'S ROOM

HEX, a large engine, or THINKING MACHINE, dominates the room. It has been draped in holly and someone has put a paper hat on the big glass dome containing the main ant heap.

The Bursar is sitting in front of the thing. Sat next to him by a large wooden keyboard is Ponder Stibbons, the Unseen University's TOKEN SANE PERSON.

>   RIDCULLY
> So, Mister Stibbons. This thing's a
> great big artificial brain, then?

Ridcully knocks the ashes out of his pipe on Hex's 'Anthill Inside' sticker, causing Ponder to wince.

>   PONDER STIBBONS
> You could think of it like that. Of
> course, Hex doesn't actually think. Not
> as such. It just appears to be
> thinking.

>   RIDCULLY
> Amazin'. You mean it gives the
> impression of thinking but
> really it's just a show?

>   PONDER STIBBONS
> Yes.

>   RIDCULLY
> Oh, so it's like everyone
> else, then, huh?

Ridcully puts his pipe back in his pocket . . . and in the process feels something else there. It's the Verruca Gnome. Ridcully pulls him out.

>   RIDCULLY
> Oh, I know I came here for
> something. Now this little
> chappie is the Verruca Gnome
> who's just popped into
> existence to be with us on
> Hogswatchnight, being the
> most magical night of the
> year. Last year's occult
> rubbish pilin' up. I thought
> you chaps might like to check
> up on it, eh?

                    PONDER STIBBONS
          The Verruca Gnome?

The gnome clutches his sack protectively.

                      RIDCULLY
          Well it makes about as much sense as
          anything else, doesn't it? After all,
          there's a Tooth Fairy, ain' there?
          Makes one wonder why there's a God of
          Wine and not a God of Hangovers . . .

He stops. There is a *glingleglingleglingle* sound.

                      RIDCULLY
          Anyone hear a noise just then?

                    PONDER STIBBONS
          Sorry, Archchancellor?

                      RIDCULLY
          Sort of *glingleglingleglingle*? Like a
          lot of tinkling bells?

                    PONDER STIBBONS
          Didn't hear anything like that, sir.

                      RIDCULLY
          Oh.

Ridcully shrugs.

                      RIDCULLY
          Well . . . where was I? . . . Oh yes
          . . . well I mean nobody's ever
          seen a Verruca Gnome until
          tonight.

                    VERRUCA GNOME
          I've never heard of me until tonight,
          and I am me.

                    PONDER STIBBONS
          Well we'll see what Hex can find out,
          Archchancellor.

                      RIDCULLY
          Good Man.

Ridcully puts the gnome back in his pocket and
looks up at Hex.

Ponder taps at the huge wooden keyboard and then nods to one of the students, who pulls a large red LEVER marked 'Do Not Pull'.

Gears spin, somewhere inside Hex. Little trap-doors open in the ant farms and millions of ants began to scurry along the networks of glass tubing . . .

> RIDCULLY (O.C.)
> Amazing. Now we should be able to get
> to the bottom of all this.

INT. DEATH'S HOUSE/LIBRARY – NIGHT

Susan blinks and thinks, and pulls a book from the shelf.

> SUSAN
> None of this is right. Everyone knows
> he's just a jolly old fat man who hands
> out presents to kids!

> RAVEN
> He wasn't always so jolly. You know how
> it is.

> SUSAN
> Do I?

> RAVEN
> Well, it's like, you know, industrial
> re-training. Even gods have to move
> with the times.

The Raven scratches at his beak.

> RAVEN
> (expansively)
> Yer see, yer Hogfather was probably
> just your basic winter demi-urge. You
> know . . . blood on the snow, making the
> sun come up.

> SUSAN
> So there has to be blood to make the
> sun come up?

Susan looks down at the book. On her face. We hear sounds: of hooves, the snap of branches in a freezing forest . . . blood.

> RAVEN (O.C.)
> Mmm, well it starts off with animal
> sacrifice, y'know, hunt some big hairy
> animal to death, that kind of stuff.
> Very folkloric, very myffic.

And then just above the book, translucent images to
match these words and sound appear: Galloping hooves,
snow on branches. Then Robes and Crowns . . .

> RAVEN (O.C.)
> Didn't stop at animals neither. They
> had sacred kings, the strongest and the
> best, died at the dark time of year to
> give life to the unconquered sun. And
> in a way the Hogfather was all of them.

Until finally . . . a bright shining ball . . .

Susan jerks awake and thrusts the book aside. The
images are gone. She opens the next book, which looks
as though it is made of strips of bark.

> SUSAN
> And then?

> RAVEN (O.C.)
> (very fast)
> And then some bright spark thought,
> 'hey, looks like that damn sun comes up
> anyway, so how come we're giving those
> druids all this free grub?' The world
> moves on and he's got to find a new
> job.

> SUSAN
> So he started as an animal sacrifice to
> make the sun come up.

> RAVEN
> Exactimundo!

> SUSAN
> And now he gives out presents?

Susan looks up, thinking.

INT. CRUMLEY'S DEPARTMENT STORE - NIGHT

Mr Crumley sits on the floor and sobs.

> **VOICE OF NOBBS (O.C.)**
> Top of the evenin', squire.

He looks up blearily at the small yet irregularly uniformed figure that has addressed him thusly.

> **CORPORAL NOBBS**
> I am Corporal Nobbs of the Watch. And
> this is Constable Visit, sir.

CORPORAL NOBBS points to his colleague, CONSTABLE VISIT, a thin neatly turned out member of the WATCH. He is exotic-looking. Nobby tears off a salute. Crumley waves a shaking finger towards the Grotto.

                    VERNON CRUMLEY
          I want you to arrest him!

                    CORPORAL NOBBS
          Arrest who, sir?

                    VERNON CRUMLEY
          The Hogfather!

                    CORPORAL NOBBS
          What for, sir?

Crumley stands up in a rage.

                    VERNON CRUMLEY
          He's sitting up there as bold as brass
          in his Grotto, giving away presents!

                    CORPORAL NOBBS
          Not quite up to speed here, sir. I
          thought the Hogfather was supposed to
          give away stuff. Isn't he?

                    VERNON CRUMLEY
          But this one's an impostor!

                    CORPORAL NOBBS
          Y'know, I always thought that. I
          thought, the Hogfather spends two weeks
          sitting in a wooden grotto in some shop
          in Ankh-Morpork? At his busy time, too?
          Yeah, it's not likely.

                    VERNON CRUMLEY
          He's not the Hogfather we usually have.

                    CORPORAL NOBBS
          Oh. You mean a different imposter? Not
          the real impostor at all.

                    VERNON CRUMLEY
          Yes . . . No . . .

Corporal Nobbs is confused.

                    CORPORAL NOBBS
          Arrest the Hogfather, style of thing?

                    VERNON CRUMLEY
          Yes!

                    CONSTABLE VISIT
          On Hogswatchnight?

                            110

                    VERNON CRUMLEY
Yes!

                    CONSTABLE VISIT
For giving away presents?

                    VERNON CRUMLEY
Ha ha!

                    CORPORAL NOBBS
In front of all these kiddies?

                    VERNON CRUMLEY
Yes . . .

                    CORPORAL NOBBS
In your shop?

                    VERNON CRUMLEY
Y— do you think that might look a bit
. . . bad?

                    CORPORAL NOBBS
Difficult to see how it'd look good,
sir.

Crumley hesitates. To his horror, he realises that
Corporal Nobbs, against all expectation, has a point.

                    VERNON CRUMLEY
Could you not do it surreptitiously?

                    CORPORAL NOBBS
Oh yes, well, surreption, yes, we
could give that a try . . .

The sentence hangs in the air with its hand out.

                    VERNON CRUMLEY
           (finally getting it)
You won't find me ungrateful. Ha ha.

INT. CRUMLEY'S DEPARTMENT STORE/FIRST FLOOR – NIGHT

Nobbs and Visit approach the Grotto.

                    CONSTABLE VISIT
In Omnia we call Hogswatchnight the
Fast of St Ossory.

They stand aside as two children scuttle down the
stairs carrying a large toy boat between them.

Constable Visit visibly grimaces with disgust.

>   CONSTABLE VISIT
>   But it is not an occasion for
>   superstition and crass commercialism.

Corporal Nobbs eyes the children gloomily.

>   CORPORAL NOBBS
>   I used to hang up my stocking every
>   Hogswatch, regular. All that ever
>   happened was my dad was sick in it
>   once.

He removes his helmet. There is the sudden gleam in his
eye.

>   CORPORAL NOBBS
>   I'm going in.

INT. TOOTH FAIRY'S CASTLE/FOOT OF TOWER – DAY

Sideney buries his head back in his spell book,
muttering an incantation virtually to himself.

Suddenly the pages of his book flick over at great
speed, as if a strong gust of wind has swept by.
Sideney almost drops the book. There is the sound of
falling teeth.

From higher in the pile, teeth are
starting to jump off the pile and
fall out of the chalk circle.

Teatime looks towards the wizard.

>   MR SIDENEY
>   There seems to be a
>   thaumic surge . . . from
>   somewhere . . .

Sideney fluffs as Teatime leans in.
The wizard's thumb heads for his
mouth.

>   MR SIDENEY
>   . . . It's as if something
>   is triggering random
>   bursts of stray belief . . .

Teatime leans very close . . . and he
isn't smiling.

INT. CRUMLEY'S DEPARTMENT STORE/GROTTO - NIGHT

Now DEATH's on a roll. A SMALL GIRL is hurried away happy, tottering under the weight of a large fluffy orang-utan.

> DEATH
> IT'S THE EXPRESSION ON THEIR LITTLE
> FACES I LIKE.

> ALBERT
> Yeah. A sort of cross between fear and
> awe. They don't know whether to laugh,
> cry or wet their pants.

> DEATH
> YES. NOW THAT IS WHAT I CALL BELIEF.

DEATH turns back to the Children.

> DEATH
> NEXT! AND WHAT'S YOUR NAME, LITTLE . . .

He hesitates, but rallies, and continues . . .

> DEATH
> . . . PERSON?

> NOBBY NOBBS
> Nobby Nobbs, Hogfather.

Corporal Nobb's face crinkles as he sits on a knee much bonier than it should be.

> DEATH
> AND HAVE YOU BEEN A GOOD BO . . . A GOOD
> DWA . . . A GOOD GNO . . . A GOOD
> INDIVIDUAL?

And suddenly Nobby finds he has no control at all of his tongue.

> CORPORAL NOBBS
> 's.

Nobby's face is fixed in a grin.

INT. TOOTH FAIRY'S CASTLE/FOOT OF TOWER - NIGHT

Hundreds of teeth are now jumping from the pile and out of the circle. The gang are frantically brushing the teeth back in.

Teatime backs Sideney, who has his thumb in his mouth,
towards the pile.

                         TEATIME
                 (smiling)
            So why isn't it working?

Sideney leans back, nervously and then looks down.

                        MR SIDENEY
            Ah . . . the chalk just got a bit
            scuffed, you know, when we were piling
            up the . . .

He can't bring himself to say it.

                        MR SIDENEY
             . . . the things.

                         TEATIME
            Are you sure that's what it is?

                        MR SIDENEY
            Well, er . . .

                         TEATIME
            What about the spell?

                        MR SIDENEY
            Oh, that'll go on for ever. The simple
            ones do. It's just a state change,
            powered by the . . . the . . . it just
            keeps going . . .

He swallows and raises a shaking arm again.

                         TEATIME
            Well that's very good, Mr Sideney,
            because if this sympathetic magic
            doesn't work, you will find me very . . .
            unsympathetic.

Sideney sucks on his thumb, hard.

INT. CRUMLEY'S DEPARTMENT STORE/STAIRS – NIGHT

Corporal Nobbs barges his way through the crowds
carrying a very large and unusually shaped present.

He only stops when he is fielded by Constable Visit.

                    CONSTABLE VISIT
            What happened? What happened?

Nobbs shows Constable Visit the present. Visit looks
horrified.

                    CONSTABLE VISIT
            It's disgusting, this whole business.
            It's the worship of idols . . .

Nobbs claws at the raven-bedecked paper to reveal . . .

                    CORPORAL NOBBS
            It's a genuine Burleigh and
            Stronginthearm double-action triple-
            cantilever crossbow with a polished
            walnut stock and silver engraved
            facings!

It finally dawns on Constable Visit that something
behind him is amiss.

                    CONSTABLE VISIT
            Aren't we going to arrest this
            impostor, corporal?

Corporal Nobbs looks blearily at him through the mists
of possessive pride.

                    CORPORAL NOBBS
            You're foreign, Washpot. I can't expect
            you to know the real meaning of
            Hogswatch.

EXT. SKY - NIGHT

The sleigh soars into the snowy sky. Albert finally
gets the roll-up in his mouth and tries to light it.

                         DEATH
            ON THE WHOLE, I THINK THAT WENT VERY
            WELL, DON'T YOU?

                         ALBERT
            Yes, master.

                         DEATH
            AND I THINK I'VE GOT THE LAUGH WORKING
            REALLY WELL NOW. HO. HO. HO.

                              ALBERT
          Yeah, sir, very jolly. Tomorrow morning
          they'll believe, all right.

                              DEATH
               (suddenly grave)
          THEY'D BETTER, BECAUSE IF THEY DON'T ...
          THEN THERE WON'T BE A TOMORROW MORNING
          . . .

And with that DEATH snaps the reins . . . just as
Albert's roll-up is finally alight. Before he can take
a puff it's blown clean out of his mouth.

The HOGS surge and pull the sleigh off into the sky.

INT. DEATH'S HOUSE/LIBRARY - NIGHT

Blood and hooves flicker in front of Susan's face from
the scroll.

                              SUSAN
          So, for the sun to come up tomorrow
          morning the Hogfather has to be alive.

                          RAVEN (O.C.)
          Precisemente.

                              SUSAN
          But what if he's dead?

Susan reaches out for the last book and tries to open
it at random . . . She looks down as there is a rush of
noise and distorted images: hooves, blood, snow,
Massive Bones of Ice and night . . .

INT. GAITER'S HOUSE/SCHOOL ROOM - NIGHT

A pair of HOGFATHER BOOTS bearing tusks that curl up
from the sole at the front land with a thump on a rug.
A sack of presents clumps down next to them.

INT. GAITER'S HOUSE/TWYLA'S BEDROOM - NIGHT

We hear a distant thump. A small hand and then Twyla's
face emerges from under the blankets. She hears another
bumping sound from downstairs.

Gawain stirs. They both look towards their door and
listen.

INT. TOOTH FAIRY'S CASTLE/FOOT OF TOWER – DAY

Sideney waves his wand with a final flourish of his arms towards the pile of teeth.

There is a pause as the gang look on. Nothing seems to be happening.

> TEATIME
> And this was going to be your big moment.

Sideney's thumb heads for his mouth.

INT. DEATH'S HOUSE/LIBRARY – NIGHT

Susan is suddenly THROWN BACK against the wall. The book drops and slams shut.

The Raven's feathers are ruffled.

Susan is slumped against the book case.

INT. GAITER'S HOUSE/SCHOOL ROOM – NIGHT

A red-gloved hand picks up a pork pie, but as it does it knocks over a glass of sherry. The glass falls in SLOW MOTION, spilling the amber liquid over a letter to the Hogfather . . .

INT. GAITER'S HOUSE/TWYLA'S BEDROOM – NIGHT

Twyla and Gawain in their pyjamas creep towards the nursery. They hear a smash of glass and stop.

> TWYLA
> (excited)
> It's him!

INT. TOOTH FAIRY'S CASTLE/FOOT OF TOWER – DAY

> TEATIME
> Such a shame.

The gang look away from Sideney, preparing to wince.

119

BANJO (O.C.)
Pretty lights.

Banjo is still looking at the teeth, his mouth gaping open.

Starting at the bottom of the pile, the teeth are starting to GLOW . . . magically.

Sideney's thumb drops from his mouth, which begins to smile.

Teatime turns towards the teeth.

TEATIME
Think happy, Banjo.

Banjo smiles on command . . . and so does Teatime.

INT. DEATH'S HOUSE/LIBRARY - NIGHT

Susan is lying prostrate. The Raven is standing on her forehead with his beak poised above one of her eyeballs. He shrugs his shoulders.

Just as he raises his head . . .

Susan's eyes slam open. The Raven jumps in the air.

RAVEN
Wake up! Wake up! You've got to find the Hogfather.

Susan rubs her head then looks down gravely at the book.

SUSAN
He was at the Castle of Bones.

She gets up, goes over to the desk and picks up DEATH's sword. Its thin blue blade flashes through the air.

INT. GAITER'S HOUSE/SCHOOL ROOM - NIGHT

Twyla and Gawain peek their heads around the door.

The figure in the red fur coat is on his knees mopping
up sherry. A small plume of smoke floats from the red
hood.

Twyla harrumphs.

> TWYLA
> You're not the Hogfather.

INT. THE CASTLE OF BONES/ENTRANCE - NIGHT

The castle looks like a giant mausoleum.

A huge piece of ice falls from the roof. It crashes
into the snow behind the columns, lifting a massive
plume of snow dust into the air.

INT. TOOTH FAIRY'S CASTLE/MONEY ROOM - NIGHT

Medium Dave Lilywhite hauls another bag of money towards the door.

> MEDIUM DAVE
> There must be thousands here . . .

> CHICKENWIRE
> What's all this stuff?

Chickenwire opens a box.

> CHICKENWIRE
> 's just paper.

He tosses it aside.

> MEDIUM DAVE
> (smirking)
> They're title deeds for properties.
> And they're better than money.

> CHICKENWIRE
> So if we steal them,
> do they become ours?

> MEDIUM DAVE
> Is that a trick
> question?

> CHICKENWIRE
> Anyway, let's get
> going. He won't miss
> a few . . .

> TEATIME
> Gentlemen . . .

They turn. Teatime is in the
doorway.

> CHICKENWIRE
> We were just er . . . we
> were just piling up
> the stuff.

Teatime laughs. Chickenwire
laughs. Even Medium Dave
laughs.

And then Teatime is on Dave, pushing him irresistibly
backwards until he hits the wall.

There is a blur. Dave tries to blink but suddenly his
left eyelid is bleeding.

Teatime's 'good' eye is close to him. The pupil is a
dot.

The knife is right by Medium Dave's face, the point of
the blade the merest fraction of an inch from his right
eye.

                    TEATIME
              (whispering)
          Ha. I know people say I'd kill them as
          soon as look at them. And in fact I'd
          much rather kill you than look at you,
          Mr Lilywhite.

He relaxes a little, but his hand still holds the
knife.

                    TEATIME
          You're thinking that Banjo's
          going to help you. That's how
          it's always been, isn't it?
          But Banjo is my friend now.

Banjo can be seen just standing there,
with a blank face.

                    TEATIME
          Banjo has the heart of a
          little child.

The others are frozen in place.

                    TEATIME
          I believe I have, too.

The knife disappears somewhere about
his clothing.

Medium Dave slumps down.

                    TEATIME
          Help him, Banjo.

On cue, Banjo lumbers forward and
helps his brother up.

TEATIME
As far as this goes . . .

He kicks a sack. It splits open. Silver and copper fall in an expensive trickle.

TEATIME
. . . I really have no use for it. It's only pillow money.

The gang watch the coins roll across the floor.

TEATIME
Something much more interesting has become apparent.

INT. THE CASTLE OF BONES/ENTRANCE - NIGHT

As snowdust drifts away in the wind we see Susan dismounting from Binky and walking into the creaking danger.

A little way beyond the pillars she finds the very large slab of ice, cracked into pieces. Far above, stars are visible through the hole it has left in the roof. As she looks up, a few small lumps of ice thump into a snowdrift.

Snow has blown over the ice. Susan looks down at the drifts. There are the faint outlines of booted footprints. And . . . half obscured by the snow . . . it looks as though a sleigh has stood here. Animals have milled around. But the snow is covering everything.

Susan bends down and finds footprints in the snow. Albert's roll-up tobacco is everywhere.

SUSAN
(to herself)
Albert. I don't see the Hogfather as someone who rolls his own.

She stands and follows the stairs into the castle.

INT. TOOTH FAIRY'S CASTLE/MONEY ROOM - NIGHT

TEATIME
Drop him.

Banjo lets his brother fall to the ground.

                         TEATIME
          Control. Control the inner child and
          it'll even give you its teeth.

The gang look at Banjo, with his gap-toothed smile.

                         TEATIME
          And somewhere in this tower you're
          going to help me find someone who can
          use it. Who can use it to give me the
          world.

He stands back and smiles happily.

Teatime goes out onto the stairs.

                      CHICKENWIRE
(whispering)
          So is he saying to take the money and
          go?

                      MEDIUM DAVE
          Don't be bloody stupid.

INT. GAITER'S HOUSE/SCHOOL ROOM – NIGHT

The figure looks over his shoulder.
The hood slips back from his head
to reveal MR GAITER, complete with
cigar.

                   GAWAIN
          (horrified)
          Daddy!

                   MR GAITER
          I say, it's not what you
          think.

On the mantelpiece the CLOCK is just
before 12. Beside it, the figure on
the Hogswatch card is entirely human
. . .

                   TWYLA
          Yes it is.

INT. TOOTH FAIRY'S CASTLE/FOOT OF TOWER - DAY

The whole of the massive pile of teeth glows a magical
glow which surges even more strongly . . .

. . . sending a wave of warm light across the faces of
the watching gang.

> TEATIME
> Mister Brown . . .

Teatime stops looking at Banjo and turns to Mr Brown.

> TEATIME
> . . . There's one door you haven't
> found. Find the Tooth Fairy's secret
> room. And when he does . . .

Mr Brown takes his bag and grumpily stumps off.

> TEATIME
> . . . then just think what I can make
> the kiddiwinkies think.

INT. THE CASTLE OF BONES/THRONE ROOM - NIGHT

Ahead of Susan a pyramid of steps, with a big chair on
top, rises majestically above her. Snow falls through a
chasm-like hole high above it.

In the snow beneath it there are a lot of Albert-shaped
footprints.

Behind her, a pillar groans and twists slightly.

Susan bends down and pulls at something half-buried in
the snow. It is a red-and-white-striped candy cane.

She kicks the snow aside elsewhere and finds a wooden
toy soldier.

She probes further and finds a broken trumpet.

There is some more groaning in the darkness.

Susan looks further into the darkness but can see
nothing.

The column nearest her creaks loudly, twists, and a
fine haze of ice crystals drops from the roof . . .
followed by a large shard of ice that crashes into the
snow right beside her.

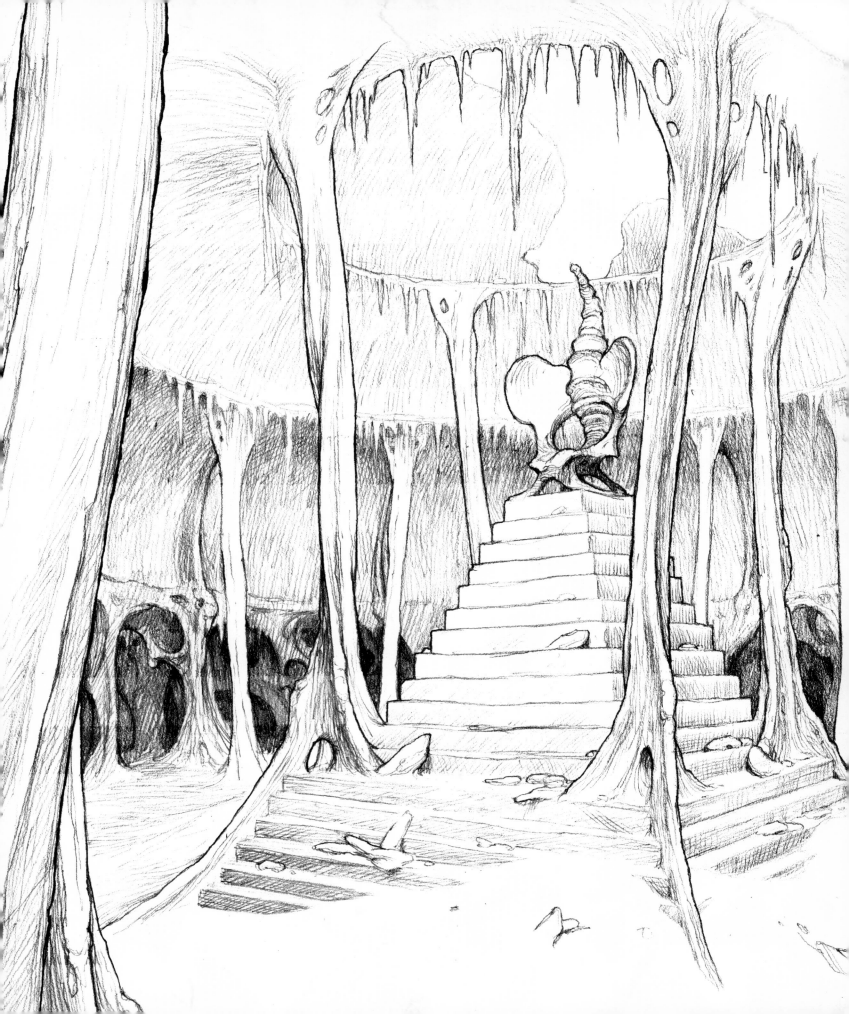

She turns to leave and hears the groan again. She stops. It isn't dissimilar to the tortured sounds being made by the ice, except that ice, after all, doesn't moan.

> VOICE IN SNOW (O.C.)
> Oh, me . . .

Susan hesitates and takes one step towards the sound.

Another shard of ice slams into the snow where she was just stood. Melt-water is now flowing from above.

Susan bites her lip and looks in the direction of the voice. Then she looks back to the way out . . . as the whole building seems to shudder and quake . . .

INT. TOOTH FAIRY'S CASTLE/FOOT OF TOWER – DAY

Teatime spins, delighted, beside the glowing pile of teeth.

INT. THE CASTLE OF BONES/THRONE ROOM – NIGHT

Susan runs . . .

. . . TOWARDS the groaning, moaning figure lying spread-eagled in a snowdrift. She almost misses it because it is only just visible in the snow.

> SUSAN
> Are you all right?

The recumbent figure opens its eyes and stares straight up.

> YOUNG MAN
> (moaning)
> I wish I was dead . . .

A piece of ice the size of a house falls down in the far depths of the building and explodes in a shower of sharp little shards.

> SUSAN
> I think you may have come to the right place.

The young man watches more falling ice and looks very, very pale.

Susan grabs the young man under his arms and hauls him
out of the snow.

She does her best to prop him up as, swaying and
slipping, they make their way back to the exit. Above
them a massive fissure opens up in the roof with a
rending, cracking sound.

                         YOUNG MAN
         My head . . .

Susan looks up and quickly back down to the young man.

                         SUSAN
              (confused)
         Are you . . . ?

Susan looks more closely at the boy.

> SUSAN
>
> . . . the Hogf—?

The ice above them creaks with a sound like thunder,
drowning Susan out. Then silence.

> YOUNG MAN
> I feel awful. Have you got any ice?

With which . . . the Castle of Bones falls in.

EXT. SKY ABOVE ANKH-MORPORK - NIGHT

DEATH urges the hogs on. Something drops into his hand.

There is a moment of horrible silence as they both
stare at the lifetimer.

DEATH looks at Albert, who looks worried.

> DEATH
>
> DUTY CALLS.

> ALBERT
> Yes, but which one?

DEATH pulls on the reins and turns the sleigh around . . .

EXT. THE CASTLE OF BONES - NIGHT

The collapse of the building is stately and impressive,
and seems to go on for a long time. Pillars fall in,
the slabs of the roof slide down, the ice crackles and
splinters. The air above the tumbling wreckage fills
with a haze of snow and ice crystals. The sound is
almost deafening.

INT. TOOTH FAIRY'S CASTLE/FOOT OF TOWER - DAY

The glowing pile of teeth is reflected in Teatime's
glass eye. As he looks up, the CAMERA cranes up,
revealing his smiling face.

> TEATIME
> Happy Hogwash, everybody.

From high above the pile, the light from the teeth
spills and bounces chaotically around the white walls.

EXT. THE CASTLE OF BONES - NIGHT

The last of the Castle of Bones collapses into rubble,
but the fate of our heroine, her mysterious new friend,
the rat and the raven . . . is unknown . . .

END OF PART 1

Terry Pratchett's
HOGFATHER
The Illustrated Screenplay

PART TWO

WRITTEN FOR THE SCREEN

BY VADIM JEAN

MUCKED AROUND WITH

BY TERRY PRATCHETT

EXT. SPACE – NIGHT

Mists roll, stars peek, glinting faintly through.

> NARRATOR (V.O.)
> Everything starts somewhere, although
> many physicists disagree. There is the
> constant desire to find out where,
> where is the point where it all
> began . . .

A star explodes, and in the distance we can just make
out an odd shape. We fly towards the Discworld.

> NARRATOR (V.O.)
> But much, much later than that . . .
> the Discworld was formed . . .

We fly around the Turtle, and the Discworld

> NARRATOR (V.O.)
> . . . drifting onwards
> through space atop four
> elephants on the shell
> of a giant turtle, The
> Great A'Tuin.

We begin to fly over the Discworld.

> NARRATOR (V.O.)
> It was some time after
> its creation when most
> people forgot that the
> very oldest stories of
> the beginning are,
> sooner or later, about
> blood . . . at least,
> that's one theory . . .

And now we're flying across the disc itself.

> NARRATOR (V.O.)
> . . . The philosopher Didactylos has
> suggested an alternative hypothesis:
> 'Things just happen. What the hell'.

And onwards over the city and down towards the
centre . . .

> NARRATOR (V.O.)
> Our story began in Ankh-Morpork, the
> twin city of proud Ankh and pestilent
> Morpork, the biggest city in Discworld

. . . a city where magic is just
another job, and where the Tower of Art
of the Unseen University for Wizards
looms over all the dark, narrow streets
below.

. . . And we continue to a street where, with a
sprinkle of magic and a *'twing'*, we appear to travel
through a narrow sparkly gate in a wall . . .

>   NARRATOR (V.O.)
> Our story continues in the middle of
> the night before Hogswatch, a mid-
> winter festival which, for some reason,
> bears a remarkable similarity to your
> Christmas . . . that now takes us to
> the Tooth Fairy's castle . . .

INT. TOOTH FAIRY'S CASTLE/FOOT OF TOWER – DAY

The tower is a hollow tube. Four spiral
staircases climb the inside, criss-
crossing on landings and occasionally
passing through one another in defiance
of generally accepted physics.

>   NARRATOR (V.O.)
> . . . where magic has made
> children's teeth perilously
> powerful, so that our story is
> much sooner, rather than later,

But . . . there is an absence of
shadows. The white marble-like stone
seems to glow from the inside. It is as
if the tower seems to avoid darkness.

>   NARRATOR (V.O.)
> . . . about blood.

INT. TOOTH FAIRY'S CASTLE/STAIRS – DAY

Teatime cranes to look up the tower.

>   MR BROWN (O.C.)
>   Mr Teh-ah-time-eh!

Mr Brown's head appears from higher up.

Teatime looks back into the room and nods to the gang to follow him. He starts up the stairs.

The gang follow.

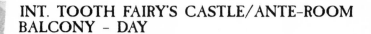

INT. TOOTH FAIRY'S CASTLE/ANTE-ROOM BALCONY - DAY

Teatime, Sideney and the gang find Mr Brown by a locked door. The locksmith's pick turns the last tumbler. Mr Brown looks through an elaborate-looking device into the lock.

                    MR BROWN
There you are. I've unlocked it.

Teatime stands back.

                    MR BROWN
And Banjo's opened it.

INT. TOOTH FAIRY'S CASTLE/TOOTH FAIRY'S ANTE-ROOM - DAY

The guard is cowering behind a pillar. He cringes back as Teatime moves towards him.

                    GUARD
        I'm not telling you anything. Who are
        you anyway?

                    TEATIME
          (cheerfully)
        I'm glad you asked. I'm your worst
        nightmare!

The guard shudders.

                    GUARD
        Oh. You . . . you mean . . . the
        one . . . the one with the . . . oh,
        with the giant cabbage and the . . .
        and the kind of whirring knife thing?

                    TEATIME
      (nonplussed)
        Sorry? No, not that one.

Teatime withdraws a dagger from his sleeve.

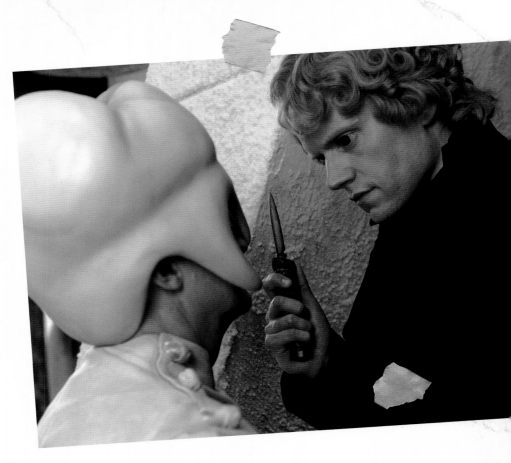

TEATIME
I'm the one where this man comes out of nowhere and kills you stone dead.

The guard grins with relief.

GUARD
Oh, that one. But that one's not very
. . .

He crumples around Teatime's suddenly outthrust fist. And then falls to the ground and fades.

TEATIME
Rather a charitable act there, I feel.

Teatime watches as the man vanishes.

TEATIME
But it is nearly Hogswatch, after all.

Teatime turns to see . . .

. . . an ordinary-looking LARGE DOOR in the wall behind the fallen cabinet. It is covered with many ELABORATE LOCKS.

Teatime smiles.

TEATIME
Bring me the girl.

EXT. ROOF TOP OF UNSEEN UNIVERSITY - NIGHT

The runners of the Hogfather's sleigh hit the roof. DEATH pulls out a Lifetimer from his cloak.

DEATH
ODD.

He looks down.

Someone, a corpse, is lying in the snow. A TOOTH-SHAPED HELMET is just about on his head. On his shirt is a badge with what looks like a DRAWING OF A TOOTH on it.

Albert looks down at the snow-covered corpse.

                    ALBERT
      Uh, it's a scythe job, then?

DEATH swings his scythe.

The spirit of the man looks down at himself. Then he stares from himself to Albert to DEATH and his phantom expression goes from shock to concern.

                  MAN'S SPIRIT
      They took the teeth! All of
      them! They just walked
      in . . . and . . .
      they . . . no, wait, wait,
      wait . . .

He fades and is gone.

Albert squints up at the sky. Then he looks around, puzzled.

                    ALBERT
      Where did he come from?

                    DEATH
      A PLACE I CANNOT GO.

Albert looks a little confused.

                    ALBERT
      No? Well, even if you could go there,
      we've got our work cut out here,
      keeping the Hogfather's seat warm.

                    DEATH
      IF WHAT'S HAPPENING IN THE TOOTH
      FAIRY'S CASTLE ISN'T STOPPED THEN
      EVERYTHING WE'VE BEEN DOING IS A WASTE
      OF TIME.

DEATH looks more closely at the
guard's tooth badge.

> DEATH
> AND IF THEY GET TO THE
> TOOTH FAIRY, THEY WILL
> BE ABLE TO CONTROL ALL
> HUMAN BELIEF.

DEATH gathers up the reins.

> DEATH
> UNLESS SUSAN GETS THERE
> FIRST.

DEATH snaps the reins and the
hogs pull the sleigh into the
night sky.

INT. UNSEEN UNIVERSITY/GREAT HALL - NIGHT

Ridcully stands in the middle
of the floor surveying the
hall.

> RIDCULLY
> Yes, well, it's coming
> along well, very
> impressive, well done.

There is a hammering on the
outer door.

The Archchancellor peers
through the spy-hole.

Then a hooded figure steps in, passing
through the closed door carrying a limp bundle over its
shoulder.

Ridcully notices that the robe has lace around the
bottom, and the hood is rather stylish, in the mode of
the classic Victorian governess.

Then the hood is pushed back. It's Susan.

> SUSAN
> I need your help, Mr Ridcully.

                    RIDCULLY
            And who are . . .
            you're . . .

                    SUSAN
            Yes, the scythe, the
            cloak, the white
            horse . . . the
            granddaughter.

                    RIDCULLY
             Oh my.

Ridcully waggles his eyebrows
towards the slumbering figure
over her shoulder.

                    SUSAN
            I need you to wake him
            up.

Ridcully lifts the oh God's
head. There's a groan.

                    SUSAN
            His name's Bilious. He's the oh God of
            Hangovers.

The wizards grimace at the thought.

                    SUSAN
            Something nasty's happening tonight.
            I'm hoping he can tell me what it is.
            But he's got to be able to think
            straight first.

                    RIDCULLY
            And you brought him here?

Susan's beginning to wonder.

INT. TOOTH FAIRY'S CASTLE/TOOTH FAIRY'S ANTE-ROOM - DAY

Teatime has his knife to Violet's throat and forces her
to look at the mysterious entrance, which is making her
so nervous she won't stop talking, so their dialogue
overlaps.

                    VIOLET
            Why are you doing this? I mean I was a
            bit behind with the teeth I know . . .

                         TEATIME
             Is she behind this door?

                         VIOLET
             I don't know . . . and there was
             nearly thirteen dollars in pillow money
             owing, I admit—

                         TEATIME
             Is this her door?

                         VIOLET
              . . . But I signed the form G-V
             nineteen for Bulk Collection and
             Despatch . . .

Teatime pushes the knife a little harder into her throat.

                         TEATIME
             Will you just shut up and answer the
             question?

Violet finally stops for a moment.

                         VIOLET
             I don't know. I've never been here
             before.

                         TEATIME
             Then your boss probably doesn't realise
             how irritating you are.

                         VIOLET
             Oh.

Teatime pushes Violet towards the door, knife still at
her throat.

                         TEATIME
             Come out, come out, wherever you
             are . . .

Another little nudge of the blade and Violet shrieks
again.

                         TEATIME
              . . . or Miss Bottler gets it.

                         VIOLET
             It was only a bit of loose change and
             I really . . . I was going to . . .

Teatime closes his eyes as Violet's terrified chatter
carries on and on . . .

EXT. SCROTE SHACK – NIGHT

The shack is pretty isolated. It is a small dot in the
middle of the Plains.

Albert is stood by the chimney, shouting down inside.

                    ALBERT
          Sam Scrote, aged eight. Have you got
          the list?

There are the clattering sounds of bone on brick from
within.

Albert's feet slip a little in the snow . . .

INT. SCROTE SHACK – NIGHT

The house has an iron stove. Voices echo faintly within
the pipe.

                    DEATH (O.C.)
          THIS IS REALLY, REALLY STUPID.

The second voice sounds as though it comes from someone
standing on the roof and shouting down the pipe.

                    ALBERT (O.C)
          I think the tradition got started when
          everyone had them big chimbleys,
          master. Ha ha.

                    DEATH (O.C.)
          INDEED? IT'S ONLY A MERCY IT'S UNLIT.

There is some muffled scratching and banging, and then
a thump from within the pot-belly of the stove. The
stove lid is lifted up and pushed sideways. A skeletal
arm with a red sleeve comes out and feels around the
front of the stove until it finds the handle. It plays
with it for a while and then opens the stove.

                    ALBERT (O.C)
          It's brass monkeys out here.

The voice sounds pitiful as it echoes down from the roof. Then there is the sound of bumping, crashing and a thump from outside the door.

The door opens and Albert enters, dusting the snow from his legs and peeling the crushed roll-up from his face.

DEATH looks at the sock hooked on to the side of the stove. It has a hole in it. A letter, in erratic handwriting, is attached to it. DEATH picks it up.

> DEATH
> THE BOY WANTS A PAIR OF TROUSERS
> THAT HE DOESN'T HAVE TO SHARE, A
> HUGE MEAT PIE, A SUGAR MOUSE, 'A LOT
> OF TOYS' AND A PUPPY CALLED SCRUFF.

> ALBERT
> Ah, sweet. I shall wipe away a tear,
> 'cos what he's gettin', see, is this
> little wooden toy and an apple.

He holds them out.

> DEATH
> BUT THE LETTER CLEARLY . . .

> ALBERT
> I know, it's socio-economic factors.
> I mean the world'd be in a hell of a
> mess wouldn't it, eh, if everyone
> got what they asked for, eh?

> DEATH
> I GAVE THEM WHAT THEY WANTED IN THE
> STORE . . .

> ALBERT
> Yeah, well what good's a god that gives
> you everything you want, huh?

> DEATH
> YOU HAVE ME THERE.

> ALBERT
> Ah, yeah, it's the hope that's
> important.

Albert gives Death the toy and apple.

ALBERT
Ooh. Oh yes, it's a big part of belief,
hope. I mean to say, you give people
jam today and they'll just sit there
and eat it. But jam tomorrow, now - ah,
no, that'll keep 'em going for ever.

DEATH
AND YOU MEAN THAT BECAUSE OF THIS THE
POOR GET POOR THINGS AND THE RICH GET
RICH THINGS?

ALBERT
Well, yeah. That's the meaning of
Hogswatch. Innit Master, eh?

DEATH nearly wails.

DEATH
BUT I'M THE HOGFATHER!

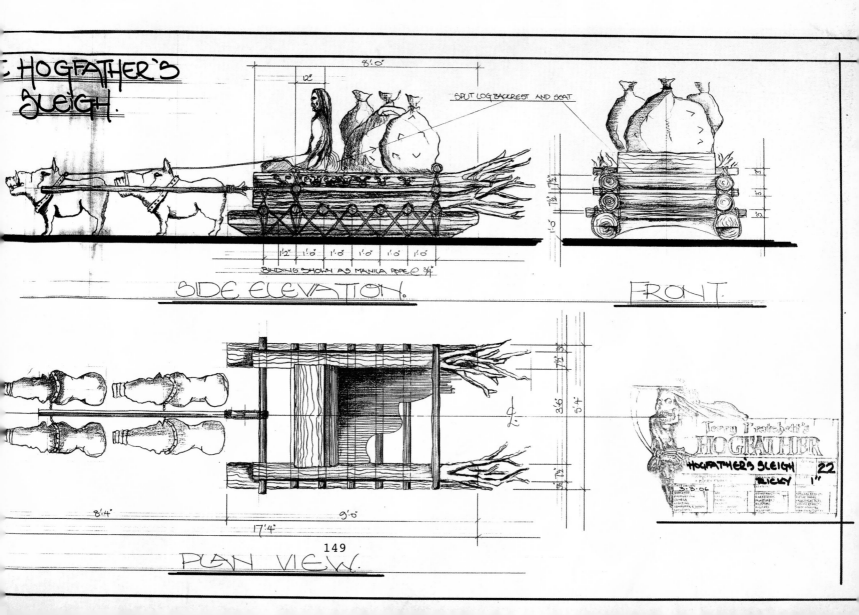

He looks embarrassed.

                    DEATH
          AT THE MOMENT, I MEAN.

Albert picks up the apple and starts to eat it.

                    ALBERT
          (shrugging)
     Well, it makes no difference. Huh, I
     remember when I was a nipper, it was
     one Hogswatch, it was I had my heart
     set on this huge model horse in this
     shop . . .

His face creases for a moment in a grim smile of
recollection. And as he does we . . .

                              DISSOLVE TO:

INT. TOYMAKER'S SHOP/PAST - DAY

. . . Albert's face as a small boy. He has his nose up
against the window. It is snowing outside.

The shop door chimes as it opens and a well-dressed
person comes in. Albert's eyes swing over to try to see
them and then back.

EXT. TOYMAKER'S SHOP - DAY

From outside we see past YOUNG ALBERT as . . .

                    ALBERT (V.O.)
     It was what I always wanted. Someone
     was in there buying it, and, y'know,
     just for a second I thought it really
     was going to be for me . . .

INT. TOYMAKER'S SHOP - DAY

The CAMERA tracks slowly in on young Albert's longing
face.

                    ALBERT (V.O.)
     But it wasn't. I spent hours with my
     nose pressed up against the

window . . . 'til someone heard me
callin', and unfroze me.

And from his face slowly we . . .

                                    DISSOLVE TO:

INT. SCROTE SHACK/PRESENT – NIGHT

Albert's face. He shrugs again.

                    ALBERT
          Huh. Yes, I would've killed for that
          horse. You know what, I still hung up
          my stocking on Hogswatch Eve, and d'you
          know why? Cos I had hope. Yeah. And the
          next morning our dad had put in my
          stocking a little wooden horse he'd
          carved his very own self . . .

                    DEATH
          AH. AND THAT WAS WORTH MORE THAN ALL
          THE EXPENSIVE TOY HORSES IN THE WORLD.

Albert starts to roll one of his horrible thin
cigarettes .

                    ALBERT
          No, 'cos you're a selfish little bugger
          when you're seven. Only grown-ups think
          like that.

Albert leans back and fiddles with his tobacco.

DEATH looks perturbed.

                    DEATH
          THIS IS WRONG. IT IS . . . UNFAIR.

Albert looks a little out of his depth at this point.

                    ALBERT
          Oh, well, that's life, innit master,
          eh.

                    DEATH
          BUT I'M NOT.
            (sadly)
          THIS IS SUPPOSED TO BE THE SEASON TO BE
          JOLLY.

He wraps his red robe around him.

                    ALBERT
          Huh?

                    DEATH
          AND OTHER THINGS ENDING IN OLLY.

Albert shakes his head.

The little ragged stocking is now bulging with a large
MEAT PIE sticking out of the top and . . . it BARKS.

INT. TOOTH FAIRY'S CASTLE/TOOTH FAIRY'S ANTE-ROOM - DAY

Medium Dave is dragging Violet out of the room.

                    TEATIME
          Please just take her out of vocal
          range.

Teatime turns to Mr Brown and indicates towards the
door.

                    TEATIME
          Mr Brown. Your big moment.

By the door, Mr Brown is sat on his tool box, which has
drawers full of hammers, picks and little chisels in it.
He is working on one of the locks. He has a STETHOSCOPE-
TYPE DEVICE in his ears as he turns a small dial.

Teatime is stood over his shoulder.

Mr Brown turns the dial one click and then smiles.

As he turns the dial again we hear the sound of bolts
falling out of place and . . . a faint hissing sound.

                    TEATIME
          Break me out the real Tooth Fairy.

INT. UNSEEN UNIVERSITY/GREAT HALL - NIGHT

The oh God moans. He is laid
out on a bench in the Great
Hall. The Senior Wizards
gather round, all eager to
help.

          BILIOUS
Ugghhh.

          RIDCULLY
Oh come along, lad.

          SUSAN
If you're the Lecturer
in Recent Runes, can't
you do something more,
well, magical?

                    LECTURER IN RECENT RUNES
          Well, Spold's Unstirring Divisor would
          do it. You'd end up with a large beaker
          filled with all the nastiness. It's not
          difficult at all, if you don't mind the
          side-effects.

                         SUSAN
            (sceptical)
          Tell me about the side-effects.

                    LECTURER IN RECENT RUNES
          Well, the main one is that the rest of
          him would end up in a somewhat larger
          beaker. Ha ha.

                         SUSAN
          Alive?

The Lecturer in Recent Runes screws up his face and
waggles his hands.

                    LECTURER IN RECENT RUNES
          Broadly, yes. Living tissue, certainly.
          And definitely sober.

Susan sighs.

                       THE DEAN
          Why don't we just mix up absolutely
          everything and see what happens?

                       RIDCULLY
          It's got to be worth a try.

Bilious twitches.

INT. UNSEEN UNIVERSITY/GREAT HALL - LATER

The big glass beaker for the cure is on a pedestal in
the middle of the floor.

The Dean drops in a GREENISH BALL OF LIGHT that sinks
under the surface. The only apparent effect is that it
bubbles and goes a darker green.

Modo tiptoes in, pushing a trolley.

                       RIDCULLY
          Ah, thank you, Modo.

There is a large metal bowl on it, in which a small
bottle stands in the middle of a heap of crushed ice.

>   SUSAN
>   Is this going to take much
>   longer? We may not have much
>   time.

>   RIDCULLY
>   Oh, you can't be too careful.

Ridcully puts down the crystal and
fishes a pair of HEAVY GLOVES from his
hat . . . and then a WELDING
MASK . . .

The wizards are suddenly no longer
gathered around Ridcully, but instead
are standing close to various items of
heavy furniture.

Ridcully carefully lifts up the bottle.

>   SUSAN
>   What's that?

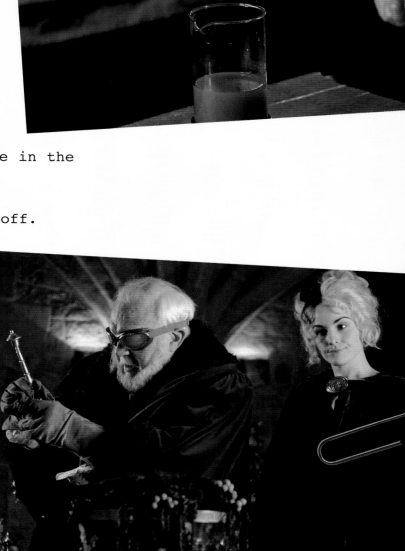

>   RIDCULLY
>   Wow-Wow Sauce. The hottest sauce in the
>   universe.

>   THE DEAN
>   And it'll blow your head clean off.

>   RIDCULLY
>   Oh, there, it's not
>   safe to drink it if
>   the sweat is still
>   condensing on the
>   bottle.

He peers at the bottle, and
then rubs at it, causing a
glassy, squeaky noise.

>   RIDCULLY
>   (brightly)
>   On the other hand, if
>   it's a kill-or-cure
>   remedy then we are,
>   given the possibility
>   that the patient is
>   immortal, probably on
>   to a winner.

155

He places a thumb over the cork and shakes the bottle vigorously.

There is a crash as the Chair of Indefinite Studies tries to get under the table.

Ridcully cautiously uncorks the bottle. There is a brief hiss of indrawn air.

The Dean and the Lecturer in Recent Runes duck down behind their heavy furniture.

Ridcully allows a few drops to splash into the beaker. Nothing happens. He sniffs suspiciously at the bottle.

                    RIDCULLY
          Wonder if it's gone critical yet?

He upturns the sauce and thumps the end. A big drop of sauce goes in and he's rewarded with a . . . GLOOP.

The wizards begin to stand up and brush themselves off, giving one another rather embarrassed grins.

Ridcully turns the bottle round, peering at it sadly. Then finally, he tips it up and thumps it hard on the base.

A trickle of sauce arrives on the lip of the bottle and glistens there for a moment. Then it begins to form a bead.

As if drawn by invisible strings, the heads of the wizards turn to look at it.

Susan, drawn by the same invisible strings, also turns to look at it.

As the bead swells and starts to go pear-shaped, the wizards turn and, with a surprising turn of speed for men so wealthy in years and waistline, dive for the floor.

The drop falls. It goes . . . GLOOP. And that is all.

Ridcully, who has been standing like a statue, sags in relief.

                    RIDCULLY
          I don't know . . .

He turns away.

>   RIDCULLY
>   I wish you fellows would show some
>   backbone . . .

The FIREBALL erupts from the POTION, lifting
Ridcully off his feet, and then rises to the
ceiling where it spreads out widely and
vanishes with a pop, leaving a perfect
chrysanthemum of scorched plaster.

INT. UNSEEN UNIVERSITY/GREAT HALL - NIGHT

Pure white light fills the room. And there is
a sound. TINKLE. TINKLE. FIZZ. (Just like
Alka-Seltzers.)

Ridcully picks himself up off the floor.

The beaker gleams. It is filled with a brown
liquid which bubbles gently.

Slowly, with the flickering light casting long
shadows on the walls, the wizards gravitate
towards the beaker.

Ridcully dips his finger into the liquid. It comes out
with one glistening drop on the end.

>   THE DEAN
>   Be careful, Archchancellor. What you
>   have there may
>   represent pure
>   sobriety.

Ridcully pauses with the finger
halfway to his lips.

>   BILIOUS
>   I'll try it.

Bilious staggers up to the
beaker, manages to grip it on
the second go, and drinks the
lot.

The oh God blinks. The wizards
watch him cautiously.
Remarkably, he seems to be
feeling better.

Bilious smiles briefly at Susan and promptly COLLAPSES.

The Dean pauses and looks at Bilious.

> THE DEAN
> You did say he was immortal, didn't you?

She bends down and slaps Bilious across the face. Nothing.

The wizards gather round the prostrate oh God.

> RIDCULLY
> And you mean . . . he just appeared?

> SUSAN
> Yes. He has no memory of existing before appearing at the Hogfather's castle.

Ridcully pulls the Verruca Gnome from his pocket.

> RIDCULLY
> You mean like this fellow.

> THE DEAN
> Oh don't be ridiculous. Gods and gnomes don't just appear en mass for no reason.

We hear the sound of a jug of water hitting flesh, followed by groaning.

A startled Bilious sits up, shakes his head and smiles.

> BILIOUS
> Ah, bring me . . . let's see . . . um, twenty pints of lager, some pepper vodka and a bottle of coffee liqueur!

Susan grabs him and pulls him over to a bench.

                    SUSAN
        I didn't have you sobered up just so
        you could go on a binge!

                    BILIOUS
        What?

                    SUSAN
        You don't drink.

                    BILIOUS
        I don't? Oh yeah.

                    SUSAN
        I need you to help me.

                    BILIOUS
        Oh.

Ridcully looks at Bilious. His face flickers as he
realises something.

                    RIDCULLY
          I'm afraid I did it, didn't I? I said
          something to young Stibbons about
          drinking and hangovers, didn't I . . . ?

                    THE DEAN
          You mean you created it just like that?
          Oh, I find that very hard to believe,
          Mustrum.

The Lecturer in Recent Runes looks at the Dean.

                    LECTURER IN RECENT RUNES
          Good job nobody mentioned the Hair Loss
          Fairy then.

The other wizards laugh.

                    THE DEAN
          I am not losing my hair! It is just
          very finely spaced.

                    LECTURER IN RECENT RUNES
          Yes, Half on your head and half on your
          hairbrush.

                    THE DEAN
       (shouting)
          For the last time, I am not . . .

He stops. There is a *glingleglingleglingle* noise.

                    RIDCULLY
          I wish I knew where that was coming
          from.

Ridcully considers for a minute.

                    RIDCULLY
          We need a bigger brain on this.

INT. UNSEEN UNIVERSITY/HEX'S ROOM – NIGHT

The door to the room is thrown open and Ridcully
enters. Ponder doesn't even turn round.

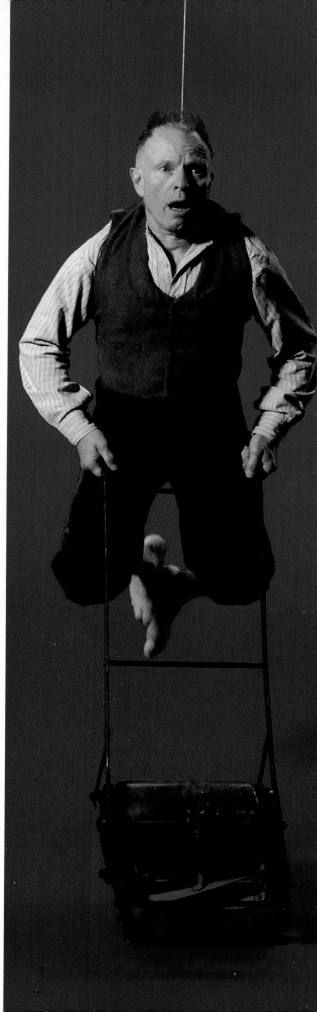

RIDCULLY
That thinking engine of yours
working, Ponder?

PONDER STIBBONS
Er, Hex is resting,
Archchancellor.

Ridcully bangs his pipe on HEX's listening tube.

RIDCULLY
Oh. CAN YOU HEAR ME IN THERE?

The pen scratches.
+++ *Yes* +++

PONDER STIBBONS
You don't have to shout,
Archchancellor.

RIDCULLY
What is this
glingleglingleglingleglingle
noise all about?

Wheels turn, ants scurry, cogs whirr around and
Hex's quill quivers into life. Ridcully reads the
text.

RIDCULLY
It says, 'Look at the Dean!' Look
at the Dean!

The other wizards turn and stare at the Dean.

Something is moving under his hat. Very
carefully, he reaches up and removes it. A very
SMALL GNOME is pushing a TINY LAWN MOWER across
his head. The little creature stops, looks up,
and blinks guiltily in the light.

HAIR LOSS FAIRY
Is there a problem?

Susan grabs it.

SUSAN
Are you the Hair Loss Fairy?

HAIR LOSS FAIRY
Apparently.

The gnome wriggles in her grip.

The Dean runs his hands desperately through his hair.

> THE DEAN
> What have you been doing with my hair?

> SUSAN
> Just a minute.

Susan turns to Bilious.

> SUSAN
> Where exactly were you
> before I found you in
> the snow?

> BILIOUS
> Anywhere where drink had
> been consumed in beastly
> quantities some time
> previously, you could
> say.

> RIDCULLY
> Ah-ha. You were an
> imminent vital force,
> eh?

> BILIOUS
> Oh. Sounds great. What
> is that?

> RIDCULLY
> So . . . when we joked about the Hair
> Loss Fairy it suddenly focused on the
> Dean's head . . .

> SUSAN
> You're calling things into being.

> BURSAR
> (cheerfully)
> I personally have always wondered if
> there was an Eater of Socks. You know
> how there's always one missing?

The wizards give this some thought. Then they all hear
it . . . *glingleglingleglingle* - the little crinkly
tinkling noise of magic taking place.

The Dean points dramatically skywards.

                         THE DEAN
              To the laundry!

The wizards surge out excitedly, leaving Susan, the oh
God, and . . . Ridcully. He shakes his head.

                         BILIOUS
              Tell me again who these people are.

                         SUSAN
              Some of the cleverest men in the world.

                         BILIOUS
              And I'm sober, am I?

Ridcully and Susan exchange a look . . .

And just at that point a young student wizard crashes
drunkenly through the gable window from the roof and
practically falls over. On his head he wears the
guard's tooth-shaped helmet.

                         RIDCULLY
              What is that ridiculous thing on your
              head?

The student tilts his eyes up to his headgear.

                    STUDENT WIZARD
                 (slurring)
              I dunno, sir.

With which he falls flat on his face. The
helmet rolls off his head and over to
Bilious, who picks it up and looks inside
the helmet.

                         SUSAN
              What? What is it?

He reads a label inside the rim.

                         BILIOUS
              It says here: 'If found please
              return to the Tooth Fairy's
              castle'.

He looks up, confused.

                         RIDCULLY
              Well, thank goodness the Tooth
              Fairy already exists, eh?

                        BILIOUS
            (thinking)
            Tooth Fairy?

                        SUSAN
            Oh, you see her around a lot these
            days, or them, rather. It's a sort
            of franchise operation to collect
            children's teeth in exchange for
            money.

                        BILIOUS
            And she has a castle? She sounds great!

Bilious looks at the helmet again.

                        BILIOUS
            Actually I do remember one thing.

Susan turns towards him.

                        BILIOUS
            When I appeared at the Hogfather's
            house there was a drunken little fellow
            in a pointy hat. I thought it was just
            the drink talking, but he did mention
            something about the . . .

INT. CASTLE OF BONES/THRONE ROOM – NIGHT

FLASHBACK to the Pixie Helper, who is now in serious
mode.

                        PIXIE HELPER
            . . . permanent end of perpetual
            servitude for the little helpers of all
            fantasy personifications . . . Ha ha!

INT. UNSEEN UNIVERSITY/HEX'S ROOM – NIGHT

                        BILIOUS
            . . . including the Tooth Fairy . . .

Ridcully takes the helmet from Bilious, hurries over to
the student and kicks him awake.

                        RIDCULLY
            Yep, yep, yep, yep, yep. Where did you
            find this?

The student groggily points towards the window he came
in through.

Susan looks at Ridcully. At last, maybe something.

They hurry to the window.

EXT. UNSEEN UNIVERSITY/ROOF – NIGHT

Susan, Ridcully and Bilious all poke their heads out of
the small gable window and look across the roof.

A dead Tooth Fairy's guard is slumped in the snow.

> BILIOUS (O.C.)
> Is he alright?

INT. UNSEEN UNIVERSITY/HEX'S ROOM – NIGHT

The group come back in. Ridcully hurries over to Hex.

Ridcully leans into Hex's speaking tube . . .

> RIDCULLY
> I say, what is the geographical
> location of the Tooth Fairy's castle?

INT. UNSEEN UNIVERSITY/CORRIDOR – NIGHT

Susan strides fast down the corridor.
Bilious is running to try to catch her.

> BILIOUS
> Now I'm feeling normal, can I
> come with you?

He catches up with Susan.

> SUSAN
> This is not a normal
> situation. Look . . .

Susan takes a big breath.

> SUSAN
> Look, I think I'd better tell
> you . . . My grandfather is
> DEATH.

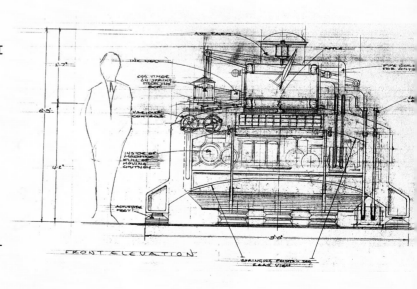

> BILIOUS
> Oh, I'm sorry to hear that.

> SUSAN
> DEATH. You know . . . DEATH? The robes,
> the . . . the scythe, the white horse,
> the bones . . . DEATH. But at the
> moment he's acting rather strange.

> BILIOUS
> I just wanna make sure I've got this
> clear. You think your grandfather is
> Death and you think he's acting
> strange?

Bilious looks at her. Susan's eyes seem to have dark
eye shadow around them. She hesitates, then as if by
rote . . .

> SUSAN
> Look, DEATH adopted my mother, he then
> took on a human apprentice, they fell
> in love and I'm the result.

> BILIOUS
> This is fascinating.

> SUSAN
> Let's just say I picked up a few
> strange genetic knacks along the way.

Susan walks through a big door. Bilious bumps into it.

EXT. UNSEEN UNIVERSITY/OCTANGLE - NIGHT

Susan emerges from the building. Binky is waiting in the
Octangle. Susan goes over to him.

Behind her Bilious finally heaves the door open and
runs after her.

Susan reaches under her coat. Her wrist moves. A
sparkling blue line flashes in the air, for a moment
outlining an edge too thin to be seen. Susan is holding
Death's sword.

The oh God backs away.

> BILIOUS
> Now that looks dangerous.

Susan sheathes the sword.

                    SUSAN
        I hope so.

Binky starts to trot but, just before he's about to
leave the ground, Bilious jumps up behind her on the
horse.

                    BILIOUS
        Wait, I could help you.

Susan groans and looks back.

                    SUSAN
        Would you be any good in a fight?

                    BILIOUS
        Yes. I could be sick on people.

And with that, Binky leaps into the air.

INT. UNSEEN UNIVERSITY/LAUNDRY ENGINE ROOM – NIGHT

Ridcully enters. The wizards are gathered
around something.

The Dean is trying to grab the Hair
Loss Fairy from under his hat.

The wizards have found the Eater of
Socks.

    CHAIR OF INDEFINITE STUDIES
            (uncertainly)
        Shoo?!

A striped proboscis sucks the
Chair of Indefinite Studies' boot
off his foot.

The boot flies past his head.

The EATER OF SOCKS looks like a
very SMALL ELEPHANT with a very
wide, flared trunk. It sucks the
sock off the wizard's foot, stuffs it
in its mouth.

EATER OF SOCKS
. . . grnf, grnf . . .

CHAIR OF INDEFINITE STUDIES
There he is . . . Catch him then!

The wizard makes a grab for it.

The wizards chase the Sock Eater behind one of the
boilers.

The Verruca Gnome chases the Chair of Indefinite
Studies' bare feet. The wizard tries to put his foot
into a big WASHING ENGINE in an attempt to keep it away
from the creature.

It is pandemonium.

RIDCULLY
Gonna have to sort this out. Can't have
creatures just popping into existence
just cos people are talking.
Unhygienic.

The Dean, hatless and sockless, shuffles past
unhappily.

INT. UNSEEN UNIVERSITY/HEX'S ROOM - NIGHT

Ridcully shouts into Hex's listening tube.

RIDCULLY
So what is this Implied Creation, then?

Hex's quill pen scratches away . . .

*+++ Humans Have Always Ascribed
Random, Seasonal, Natural Or
Inexplicable Actions To Human-Shaped
Entities. Such Examples Are The
Hogfather, The Tooth Fairy And Death
+++*

Ridcully looks up from the paper.

RIDCULLY
Well, that's all very well, but I'm
damned sure there's never been a . . .
an Eater of Socks or an oh God of
Hangovers.

Ponder Stibbons is making notes.

> **PONDER STIBBONS**
> I think it works like this. What we're getting is the personification of forces, just like Hex said.

> **RIDCULLY**
> What, like the Hogfather? And . . . and . . . and . . . When you're a kiddie it's a . . . it's as good an explanation as any of where the presents come from.

Ponder shrugs a sort of agreement.

> **RIDCULLY**
> But why has it happened now?

Ridcully and Ponder look at Hex in unison.

The sound of Hex's quill as it scrabbles across the paper is like a frantic spider trapped in a matchbox, and then it comes to a rest.

> *+++ Belief's Causing New Creatures To Appear +++*

> **RIDCULLY**
> You could put it like that.

> *+++ There's A Finite Quantity Of Belief In The Universe +++*

Ridcully looks at Ponder. He shrugs.

> **RIDCULLY**
> Well, certainly people can only believe in so many things.

> *+++ It Follows That If A Major Focus Of Belief Is Removed, That There Will Be Spare Belief +++*

Ridcully stares at the words.

> **RIDCULLY**
> All right, then, so what are people not believing in all of a sudden?

> *+++ Out Of Cheese Error +++ MELON MELON MELON +++ Redo From Start +++*

PONDER STIBBONS
It's Hogswatch. I suppose the
Hogfather is around, isn't
he?

EXT. SKY – NIGHT

DEATH is deep in thought.

DEATH
I LIKE THIS JOB.

Albert spits over the side of the sleigh and
as he does fails to see the tobacco blow out
of the cigarette paper.

ALBERT
Oh dear, oh dear, oh
dear . . .

Finally Albert lights the cigarette. He
smiles. It bursts into flames.

DEATH
EXCUSE ME . . .

DEATH reaches into his robe and pulls out a
Lifetimer. He looks at the dwindling sand and
taps the glass with a finger.

DEATH
YES. THIS WILL SHOW
THEM . . .

And the sleigh jerks down.

EXT. MONEY TRAP LANE/ANKH-MORPORK – NIGHT

DEATH and Albert in the sleigh swerve around
at the end of the street.

ALBERT
But . . . poor little match
girls dying in the snow is
all part of the spirit of
Hogswatch, master. You see,
people hear about it, and
they say, 'well, we might be
as poor as a disabled banana
and only can afford to eat

mud and boots, but see how much better off we are than the poor little match girl'. So that makes them happy and grateful for what they have got.

              DEATH
     I KNOW WHAT THE SPIRIT
     OF HOGSWATCH IS,
     ALBERT.

Albert frowns. They have reached the spot.

DEATH looks down at the shape under the falling snow. Then he lifts the Lifetimer and touches it with a finger. A spark flashes across, and the lifetimer slowly fills again.

              ALBERT
          (feeling wretched)
     You're not allowed to do that.

              DEATH
     THE HOGFATHER CAN. THE HOGFATHER GIVES
     PRESENTS. THERE'S NO BETTER PRESENT
     THAN A FUTURE.

              ALBERT
     That's it, I've had enough of this
     pixie lark.

INT. UNSEEN UNIVERSITY/LIBRARY – NIGHT

The wizards are sat in the library . . . in the dark. We can just about make out the shiny bits on their hats.

              PONDER STIBBONS
     I'm waiting for the Hogfather. I'm in
     the dark waiting for the Hogfather. Me.
     A believer in Natural Philosophy. I can
     find the square root of twenty-seven-
     point-four in my head. I shouldn't be
     doing this. It's not as if I've hung a
     stocking up. Be some point if . . .

He sits rigid for a moment, and then pulls off his
sock.

EXT. MONEY TRAP LANE/ANKH-MORPORK - NIGHT

Corporal Nobbs and Constable Visit emerge onto the
streets and tramp through the snow until they are
accosted by a tall figure.

>   DEATH
>   (commanding)
>   TAKE HER SOMEWHERE WARM AND GIVE HER A
>   GOOD DINNER.

He pushes the bundle into the arms of Constable Visit.

>   DEATH
>   AND I MAY WELL BE CHECKING UP LATER.

Then he turns and disappears into the street.

Constable Visit looks down at the little girl in his arms, pulls aside the blanket and then looks at Corporal Nobbs.

                    CORPORAL NOBBS
          Looks like we've been chosen to do a
          bit of charity.

                    CONSTABLE VISIT
          Well I don't call it very charitable,
          just dumping someone on people like
          this.

                    CORPORAL NOBBS
          I dunno. Some people wouldn't know the
          real meaning of Hogswatch if it came up
          and clocked 'em in the gob.

They trudge off into the snow anyway.

INT. TOOTH FAIRY'S CASTLE/TOOTH FAIRY'S ANTE-ROOM - DAY

Mr Brown is concentrating hard on the lock to the door, until there is a click. He looks back at the gang and a smile crosses his face.

Medium Dave and Chickenwire inch forward to see . . .

There is a rush of air releasing, as if a seal has been broken that blows the locksmith's hair back and . . .

   . . . shadows rush across his face.

                    MR BROWN
               (terrified)
          No!

EXT. A CHILD'S SKY - DAY

Binky gallops easily across . . . green . . . except that he does not seem to move.

They are riding through a child's painting. Binky stops on the grass beside the river. Or at least on the green. Susan slides off, and looks down at the vivid blue of the water.

There are orange fish in it. They are made of two curved lines and a dot and a triangular tail. She kneels down and dips her hand in. What pours through

her fingers is liquid blue. A smile crosses her face,
as if she now knows where she is.

>   SUSAN
>   This is a child's painting.

The oh God tumbles down from Binky.

>   SUSAN
>   Twyla paints like that. I painted like
>   that. Grandfather saved some of my draw—

She stops.

>   SUSAN
>   Come on, let's find the house.

>   BILIOUS
>   (moaning)
>   What house?

>   SUSAN
>   There's always a house . . .

INT. TOOTH FAIRY'S CASTLE/TOOTH FAIRY'S ANTE-ROOM – DAY

Teatime is right in Mr Brown's face. The locksmith is
stood back from the door. He looks white.

>   TEATIME
>   I was told you were the best locksmith
>   in the city.

Mr Sideney is stood like a petrified statue . . . with
his thumb in his mouth.

Teatime stares at Mr Brown with that gaze.

The locksmith looks away as a SHADOW ripples across his
face and he lays down his pick.

Mr Brown looks flustered.

>   MR BROWN
>   Yes. But locks don't generally alter
>   'emselves while you're working on 'em,
>   that's what I'm saying.

>   TEATIME
>   Are you the best or not?

Mr Brown reluctantly goes back to his work. Shadows ripple across the roof and engulf him.

                    MR BROWN
          No! Not the Dark!

Teatime turns. But Sideney has gone . . .

Medium Dave turns. So has Chickenwire . . .

The Assassin and Dave leave the room.

INT. TOOTH FAIRY'S CASTLE/FOOT OF TOWER - DAY

Banjo is sat in a hand-cart, swinging his feet contentedly looking up at the teeth where Sideney is stood.

The wizard looks up to the top of the tower to see if anyone's looking and then hurries over to Banjo.

                    MR SIDENEY
          Banjo, I'm getting out of here. There's
          something wrong with this place.

                    BANJO
            (smiling)
          I made a big pile.

                    MR SIDENEY

          Do you want to come with me?

                    BANJO
          Pretty here.

Sideney starts to move towards the door.

                    TEATIME (O.C.)
          Mr Sideney.

Sideney stops. Teatime is stood at the door. The wizard's shoulders slump.

INT. UNSEEN UNIVERSITY/LIBRARY - NIGHT

Ridcully and Ponder are still waiting in the dark for the Hogfather. Ponders sock is now hung by the chimney

                    RIDCULLY
Would he deliver to apes
earlier than to humans?

                    PONDER STIBBONS
Interesting point, sir. Possibly
you're referring to my theory
that humans may have in fact
descended from apes. A bold
hypothesis which, if the Grants
Committee could just see their
way clear to letting me hire a
boat and sail around the
islands . . .

                    RIDCULLY
I just thought he might deliver
alphabetically.

                    PONDER STIBBONS
    Oh.

There is a patter of soot in the cold
fireplace. Something lands in the ashes.

The wizards stand quietly in the darkness.

The scarcely discernible figure picks itself up. There
is a rustle of paper.

                    DEATH (O.C.)
    LET ME SEE NOW.

There is a click as Ridcully's pipe falls out of his
mouth.

Ridcully picks up his pipe.

                    RIDCULLY
    Who the hell are you?

DEATH backs away.

The wizards are waiting for a response from DEATH.

                    DEATH
    I'M THE HOGFATHER, OF COURSE. UM. HO.
    HO. HO.

Ridcully looks closer.

                    RIDCULLY
You look extremely thin in the
face!

                     DEATH
I'M . . . UM . . . I'M A BIT ILL.

                    RIDCULLY
Terminally, I would say.

Ridcully grabs the beard. There is a twang
as the string gives way.

                    RIDCULLY
Ah ha! It's a false beard!

                     DEATH
                (desperately)
NO IT'S NOT.

                    RIDCULLY
It's got hooks for the ears. That must
have given you a spot of trouble, eh?

Ridcully flourishes the incriminating evidence and
prods DEATH in the cushion with it.

>   LECTURER IN RECENT RUNES
>   It's a pillow. Ha ha.

Ponder looks horrified.

EXT. A CHILD'S PAINTING - DAY

Susan pulls Bilious along and suddenly they are out of
the trees. There, by a bend in the river, is the HOUSE.

It doesn't look very big. There are four windows and a
door. Corkscrew smoke curls out of the chimney.

Susan hesitates and then they start to walk towards
it . . .

INT. TOOTH FAIRY'S CASTLE/TOOTH FAIRY'S ANTE-ROOM - DAY

Mr Brown is still working at one of the locks.

>   TEATIME
>   I thought there were seven locks?

>   MR BROWN
>   Yes, but . . . they're half magic and
>   half real and half not there . . . I
>   mean . . . there's part of them that
>   don't exist half the time . . .

>   TEATIME
>   And I thought you could open any lock
>   anyone ever made.

>   MR BROWN
>   (sharply)
>   Made by humans. And most dwarfs. Dunno
>   what made these. You never said
>   anything about magic.

The locksmith gives the lock a frustrated bang with his
fist and then turns to face Teatime. There is a hissing
sound from the lock.

>   TEATIME
>   That's a shame. Then really I have no
>   more need of your services. You may as
>   well go back home.

Mr Brown starts putting things back into his tool bag.

                    MR BROWN
          What about my money?

                    TEATIME
          Of course, you should get what you
          deserve.

     Banjo lumbers forward, and then stops.

     Mr Brown's hand comes out of the bag holding a crowbar.

                    MR BROWN
          You must think I was born yesterday, Mr
          Teacup. I'm leaving, right? With what's
          coming to me. And you ain't stopping
          me. Banjo certainly ain't. I knew his
          old Ma in the good old days.

     Mr Brown glares at Teatime, flourishing the crowbar.

                                        MR BROWN
                                   You think you're
                                   nasty? You think
                                   you're mean? Ma
                                   Lilywhite'd tear your
                                   ears off and spit 'em
                                   in your eyes, you
                                   cocky little devil.

                              Banjo lifts Mr Brown up by the
                              scruff of his neck. He struggles
                              in mid-air.

                                        MR BROWN
                                   I remembers you when
                                   you was little, Banjo,
                                   I used to sit you on
                                   my knees
                                        . . .

                              Teatime snaps his fingers.

                              From the crack around the door
                              DARK SHADOWS seep out and then
                              rush across the walls as we hear
                              the sounds of Mr Brown
                              struggling.

INT. TOOTH FAIRY'S CASTLE/ROOM – NIGHT

Medium Dave comes into the room. Chickenwire is hiding
in a corner.

                    MEDIUM DAVE
    There you are.

                    CHICKENWIRE
    Where's all these shadows coming from?
    It's giving me the creeps and it's all
    your fault.

                    MEDIUM DAVE
    Oh, yeah? So it wasn't you who said,
    'Wow, ten thousand dollars, count me
    in'?

                    CHICKENWIRE
    Yeah, but I didn't know there was going
    to be all this creepy stuff! I want to
    go home!

                    MEDIUM DAVE
    It's like dealing with a chil—

Then, high above them . . . a scream. It goes on for a
while and seems to be getting nearer. Then it stops and
is replaced by a rush of thumping and an occasional
sound like a coconut being bounced on a stone floor.

Medium Dave opens the door . . . just in time to see
the body of Mr Brown the locksmith tumble past, moving
quite fast and not at all neatly.

Mr Brown's bag of tools somersault around the curve of
the stairs. It splits and there is a jangle as crowbars
and lockpicks bounce out and follow their late owner.

                    MEDIUM DAVE
    Er . . . poor guy must've slipped.

                    CHICKENWIRE
    Oh, yeah . . . slipped.

Chickenwire looks up. There are shadows, moving across
the stone. In the stone.

Medium Dave looks up too. Two turns of stairs above
him, on the opposite side of the huge shaft, Banjo is
watching him.

I/E. TOOTH FAIRY'S CASTLE/ENTRANCE HALL - DAY

                    BILIOUS
          That's the Tooth Fairy's castle?

As Susan and Bilious get closer we realise that the
child's house is actually quite small. At the door
Susan turns the doorknob and crouches down to go in.

Inside, the oh God gasps. The building is enormous.

The staircases start opposite one another in what is
now a big round tower, its ceiling lost in the haze.
The spirals circle into infinity.

Susan's eyes go to a large conical heap in the middle
of the floor. It is white and glistens in the cool
light that shines down from the mists.

                    SUSAN
          It's teeth.

                BILIOUS
          (looking faint)
          And I should be scared?

                              SUSAN
                    There's nothing that
                    scary about teeth.

                From Susan's face as she looks
                at, it's clear she doesn't mean
                it.

                The heap is very horrible indeed.

                              BILIOUS
                    Did I say I was scared?
                    I must just be hung-over
                    again . . .

                Susan advances on the heap, moving
                warily.

                They are small teeth. Children's
                teeth. A chalk mark has been drawn
                around the obscene heap.

                She stares down at the chalk marks.

                              BILIOUS
                    They're only teeth.

Voices high above her make Susan look
up. She catches a quick glimpse of a
head looking over the stair rail, and
then drawing back again. It doesn't
look very fairylike.

She glances back at the circle of chalk
around the teeth.

There are a few symbols scrawled around
the circle.

           SUSAN
      Surely no one would try
      to . . .

           BILIOUS
      What is that?

           SUSAN
    (sighing)
      It's such old magic it isn't
      even magic any more. If you've
      got a piece of someone's hair, nail
      clipping, or tooth, you can control
      them. Don't tell me someone's . . .

The oh God tries to focus just as . . . someone
shouts, someone up in the whiteness. A shadow
flitters across the wall.

           BILIOUS
      What's that shadow?

           SUSAN
      This place is alive.

A body rolls down the stairs nearest her, then
tumbles across the white marble and slides to a
boneless halt. It's MR BROWN.

Then, as she hurries towards the body, it fades
away, leaving nothing behind but a smear of blood.

A *jingle* noise makes her look back up the
stairs. Spinning over and over, a CROWBAR bounds
over the last steps and lands point first,
staying upright and vibrating.

           SUSAN
      And it's protecting itself.

Susan stops in her tracks.

INT. UNSEEN UNIVERSITY/LIBRARY - NIGHT

Ridcully steps closer to DEATH.

> RIDCULY
> So what's happened to the other fellow?

DEATH ponders for a moment.

> DEATH
> WELL . . .

The wizards are gathered around DEATH.

> DEATH
> THE HOGFATHER HAS ENEMIES.

> RIDCULLY
> What did he do? Miss a chimney?

DEATH looks down at them and thrums his fingers on his scythe.

INT. TOOTH FAIRY'S CASTLE/TOOTH FAIRY'S ANTE-ROOM - NIGHT

Chickenwire reaches the top of the stairs, panting.

> CHICKENWIRE
> (wheezing)
> There's people down there, Mister
> Teatime!

Teatime doesn't take his eyes off the wizard.

> TEATIME
> Well? Just . . . do away with them.

> CHICKENWIRE
> Well, er . . . one of them's a girl.

Teatime still doesn't look round. He waves a hand vaguely.

> TEATIME
> Then do away with them politely.

Teatime turns to Sideney.

                            TEATIME
                    Keep going . . . quicker.

Sideney turns quickly back to his work.

Chickenwire stands there for a moment, and then hurries
off.

INT. TOOTH FAIRY'S CASTLE/LOWER STAIRS – DAY

Susan runs up a flight of stairs,
dragging the oh God behind her.

INT. TOOTH FAIRY'S CASTLE/DISPLAY CASE ROOM 3 – DAY

There are no windows to the room,
but it's lit perfectly well by the
white walls themselves. Susan and
Bilious walk down the middle of
the room alongside something like
display cases with their lids
gaping open. Bits of card litter
the floor.

INT. TOOTH FAIRY'S CASTLE/STAIRS – DAY

Chickenwire scurries down the
stairs. He hears a creak, as of an
ancient wooden door. He goes pale.
The look on his face is as if he
has had some terrible memory. He
gives a little yelp and starts to
take the stairs four at a time.

In the hollows and corners, the shadows grow darker.

INT. TOOTH FAIRY'S CASTLE/DISPLAY CASE ROOM 3 – DAY

A scream of shock. Susan turns sharply towards the
door.

                            BILIOUS
                    What was that?

                              SUSAN
                  It's finding their nightmares.

Susan throws open the door.

INT. TOOTH FAIRY'S CASTLE/BOTTOM OF TOWER - NIGHT

A trembling Chickenwire reaches the bottom of the tower
and heads straight for the door until . . .

    . . . a hand grabs him. It's Medium Dave.

                           CHICKENWIRE
                  Let me out! It's after me!

                           MEDIUM DAVE
                  Pull yourself together! Look around!
                  There's nothing's chasing you!

Chickenwire looks back up the stairs. There is nothing
there. He looks at his feet.

                           CHICKENWIRE
                      (muttering)
                  I thought it was the w-w-w-wardrobe.

                           MEDIUM DAVE
                  What wardrobe?

                           CHICKENWIRE
                  When I was a kid . . .

Chickenwire waves his arms vaguely.

                           CHICKENWIRE
                  We had this big wardrobe. It had
                  this . . . this . . . on the door it
                  had this face . . . face an' at
                  night . . .

Chickenwire's voice goes as quiet as a vole in a
dungeon.

                           CHICKENWIRE
                  . . . it whispered things.

Medium Dave squints upwards.

                           MEDIUM DAVE
                  Who's that moving up there?

INT. TOOTH FAIRY'S CASTLE/CORRIDOR - NIGHT

Susan darts off the stairs and drags the oh God along a corridor lined with white doors.

> SUSAN
> I think they saw us. And if they're
> tooth fairies there's been a really
> stupid Equal Opportunities policy . . .

She pushes open a door.

INT. TOOTH FAIRY'S CASTLE/MONEY ROOM - DAY

Susan enters and sees the open safe doors and piles of title deeds left scattered on the floor.

She crosses the passage to another room . . .

INT. TOOTH FAIRY'S CASTLE/PASSAGEWAY - DAY

Medium Dave and Chickenwire run down the passage until they come to a split of ways.

> MEDIUM DAVE
> Right. You go that way, I'll go this
> way . . .

> CHICKENWIRE
> (terrified)
> Why don't we stay together?

> MEDIUM DAVE
> What's got into you?

He walks off.

Chickenwire peers down the other passage. There aren't many doors down there. It isn't very long. He starts to walk down it. There is a distant creaking sound behind him.

INT. TOOTH FAIRY'S CASTLE/CORRIDOR - DAY

Susan and Bilious enter the corridor. Susan stops.

> SUSAN
> This is a children's place. The rules
> are what children believe.

                    BILIOUS
          Well, that's a relief.

                    SUSAN
          (ominously)
              You think so? It's impossible to die
              here. My Grandfather doesn't figure in
              a child's world.

                    BILIOUS
          That man who fell down the stairs
          looked pretty dead to me.

                    SUSAN
          Oh, you die. But not here. You . . .
          let's see . . . yes . . . you go
          somewhere else. Away.

                    VOICE (O.C.)
          I'm trapped. Hello? Hello?!

The voice comes from the door they are passing. Susan
and Bilious look at each other.

INT. TOOTH FAIRY'S CASTLE/DISPLAY CASE ROOM 1 - DAY

Susan and Bilious hurry into the room.

Sitting on the floor and tied to the leg of a white display
case, is Violet. She looks up in apprehension . . .

          Susan hurries over and rips off the gag

                    VIOLET
          Aren't you Sus . . . ?

                    SUSAN
          Yes, yes and when you came for
          Twyla's last tooth you were so
          shocked that I could see you . . .

                    VIOLET
          (Interrupts)
          Oh yes, and I saw . . .

Susan fumbles with the ropes. Violet keeps talking.

                    SUSAN
          (Interrupts)
          Look, we may not have a lot of time.

Is this the Tooth Fairy?

SUSAN
A Tooth Fairy.

The oh God looks at Violet and tries
to push his lank hair into place. He
has the glazed look of one smitten.

BILIOUS
Do you drink at all?

Violet looks confused, but unable to
take her doe eyes from Bilious.

VIOLET
No, I don't!

The oh God raises his eyebrows at
Susan.

BILIOUS
Not touch alcohol at all?

VIOLET
Never! My dad's very strict about that
sort of thing!

Now Bilious looks really besotted.

BILIOUS
Nice castle.

After a moment Susan feels forced to wave a hand across
their locked gaze.

SUSAN
Can we get on?

Their gaze breaks reluctantly. The oh God helps her on
to her feet.

SUSAN
Good. Who brought you here, Violet?

VIOLET
I don't know! But he's dressed like an
Assassin.

Susan looks dubiously at the two of them.

                    SUSAN
OK. You stay here, I'll go and
find him . . .

                    BILIOUS
   . . . And I'll look after
Violet.

Susan leaves the room.

INT. TOOTH FAIRY'S CASTLE/TOOTH FAIRY'S ANTE-ROOM - DAY

Teatime watches over Sideney as he puts a green filter over his lantern and presses down on the lock with a small silver rod that has an emerald set on its tip. A piece of the lock moves. There is a whirring from inside the door and something goes click. He sags with relief.

                    MR SIDENEY
That's the fourth lock open.

                    TEATIME
I commend your expertise. And the
others?

Sideney looks up nervously at the silent bulk of Banjo, and licks his lips. There is a hissing sound and the wizard looks back down.

A wisp of vapour oozes from the crack between the door and the frame.

                    MR SIDENEY
Do you know exactly what's in here,
Mister Teh-ah-time-eh?

                    TEATIME
Logically, if you are the guardian of
children's beliefs and this is your
castle and I come across as securely
locked a door as this, then not to
thoroughly investigate would . . .

Teatime searches carefully for the word . . .

192

> TEATIME
> . . . lack elegance.

Sideney looks up, fear in his eyes.

> MR SIDENEY
> What's that sound . . . ?

> TEATIME
> What sound?

> MR SIDENEY
> That sound . . . like old scissors
> scraping . . .

The wizard's thumb moves slowly to his mouth.

INT. UNSEEN UNIVERSITY/LIBRARY - NIGHT

DEATH steeples his long bony fingers in
front of him.

> DEATH
> HAVE YOU EVER HEARD OF THE
> AUDITORS?

> RIDCULLY
> I wouldn't . . . I suppose the
> Bursar might have done . . .

> DEATH
> NOT AUDITORS OF MONEY. AUDITORS OF
> REALITY. THEY ARE THE CIVIL
> SERVICE OF EVERYTHING.

Ponder Stibbons grimaces at the thought.

> RIDCULLY
> And they want to get rid of us?

> DEATH
> THEY WANT HUMANS TO BE . . .
> LESS . . . CREATIVE. THE
> HOGFATHER IS A SYMBOL OF
> THIS . . .

DEATH cracks his knuckles his fingers,
causing echoes to bounce off the walls.

                              DEATH
            . . . STRANGE THINKING.
            THEY HATE THE WAY HUMANS
            MAKE UP STORIES ABOUT THE
            UNIVERSE.

                              RIDCULLY
            I can't think why. Anyway,
            why . . . why're you doing
            this job?

                              DEATH
            SOMEONE MUST. IT IS VITALLY
            IMPORTANT. BEFORE DAWN,
            THERE MUST BE ENOUGH BELIEF
            IN THE HOGFATHER.

                       RIDCULLY

      Why?

                       DEATH
            SO THAT THE SUN WILL COME UP.

      The wizards laugh.

                       DEATH
            I SELDOM JOKE.

      They gather their thoughts.

INT. TOOTH FAIRY'S CASTLE/CORRIDOR – DAY

Violet and the oh God amble down the stairs.

                       VIOLET
            What sort of Godding do you do?

Violet is round-eyed with fascination.

                       BILIOUS
            Oh, I'm the, er . . . I'm the Oh God
            of Hangovers.

                       VIOLET
            A God of Hangovers? Oh, how awful!

                       BILIOUS
            I suppose so.

                    VIOLET
          You're more cut out to be one of
          those important gods.

Bilious is smitten. But suddenly someone
is behind him holding a WIRE tight to his
throat.

                  CHICKENWIRE
          What's this? Lover's Lane?

                    VIOLET
          You leave him alone, you! He's a
          god!

Bilious swallows, gasping. But out of the
corner of his eye he can see shadows moving
very fast across the walls.

Chickenwire is looking jittery.

                  CHICKENWIRE
          Dear me, out of thunderbolts, are
          we? Well, y'know, I've never killed
          a god . . .

There is a creak.

Chickenwire's face is a few inches from Bilious. The
thief's eyes roll. His lips say 'nur . . .' like a
child.

Bilious risks stepping away. Chickenwire's grip loosens
on the wire. He stands there, trembling slightly. The
oh God looks up at the thing on the landing above.

It is just a wardrobe. Dark oak, a bit of fancy
woodwork glued on.

Chickenwire's garrotte falls to the floor.

He takes a step backwards up the stairs, but very
slowly, and then spins round.

Bilious looks on in shocked amazement.

Chickenwire just revolves, as if some giant hand has
been placed on his head and twisted a hundred and
eighty degrees. He is level with the lock on the
wardrobe door.

The lock has decoration around the keyhole which at
first looks like flowers and leaves, but looked at in
the right way there is a face . . .

. . . and Chickenwire is looking at it in exactly the
right way . . .

The doors of the wardrobe swing open.

Chickenwire manages to thrust out his arms and grab the
sides and, for a moment, he stands quite still.

> BILIOUS
> What's the matter?

In one sudden movement Chickenwire is pulled into the
wardrobe and the doors slam shut.

The little brass key turns in the lock with a click.

The oh God runs up the steps to the wardrobe. He turns
the key and opens the doors.

> BILIOUS
> It's just a wardrobe, isn't it?

> VIOLET
> I don't want to see! I don't want to see!

Violet looks over his shoulder.

Bilious reaches down and picks up a pair of boots that
stand neatly in the middle of the wardrobe's floor.

Then he puts them back carefully and walks around the
wardrobe. It is plywood. He looks closer.

The words *Dratley and Sons, Phedre Road, Ankh-Morpork*
are stamped in one corner in faded ink.

INT. UNSEEN UNIVERSITY/LIBRARY - NIGHT

> PONDER STIBBONS
> Hex was right, Archchancellor.

> DEATH
> HEX? WHO IS HEX?

> PONDER STIBBONS
> Er . . . He is the biggest thinker in
> the world.

DEATH drums the tips of his fingers together,
thoughtfully.

                    DEATH
          I WOULD LIKE TO MEET THIS MR HEX.

At which point there is a scream of horror from a
cupboard.

The wizards hurry over and open it. The reason for the
scream is lying on the floor. It's Chickenwire's dead body.

Ridcully pushes his way through the crowd.

                    RIDCULLY
          Ye gods.

The face of the corpse looks as though it died of
fright.

Ridcully looks at the feet. It has no boots on.

The Dean takes a small glass cube from his pocket and
runs it over the corpse.

                    THE DEAN
          Quite a large thaumic reading,
          gentlemen. I think he got here by
          magic.

Ridcully looks around for DEATH . . . who is not there.

                    RIDCULLY
          Where did he go?

INT. UNSEEN UNIVERSITY/HEX'S ROOM - NIGHT

DEATH looks up at Hex. The points of blue light in his
sockets flare.

                    DEATH
          THEY SAY YOU ARE THE BIGGEST THINKER IN
          THE WORLD. BUT DO YOU ALSO BELIEVE?

HEX scribbles:

          +++ Yes +++

                    DEATH
          EXTEND LOGICALLY THE RESULT OF THE
          HUMAN RACE CEASING TO BELIEVE IN THE
          HOGFATHER. WILL THE SUN COME UP?

ANSWER.

The wheels spin. The ants run. The mouse squeaks. An eggtimer comes down on a spring. It bounces aimlessly for a while, and then jerks back up again.

HEX writes:

> +++ *The Sun Will Not Come Up* +++

                          DEATH
CORRECT. HOW MAY THIS BE PREVENTED? ANSWER.

> +++ *Regular and Consistent Belief* +++

                          DEATH
GOOD. I HAVE A TASK FOR YOU, THINKING ENGINE. BELIEVE IN THE HOGFATHER.

                          DEATH
DO YOU BELIEVE? ANSWER.

                          DEATH
DO . . . YOU . . . BELIEVE? ANSWER.

> +++ *YES* +++

There is a change in the ill-assembled heap of pipes and tubes that is Hex. The big wheel creaks into a new position. From the other side of the wall comes the hum of busy bees.

                          DEATH
GOOD.

DEATH turns to leave the room, but stops when Hex begins to write furiously. He goes back and looks at the emerging paper.

> +++ *Dear Hogfather, For Hogswatch I Want* . . . +++

                          DEATH
OH, NO.

DEATH waits until the pen has stopped and picks up the paper. He reads the list, groans and then rummages in his sack.

                          DEATH

OH, LET ME SEE . . . HOW OLD ARE YOU?

DEATH leans in to the workings.

> DEATH
> AND HAVE YOU BEEN NAUGHTY . . . OR
> NICE?

INT. TOOTH FAIRY'S CASTLE/STAIRS BY TF'S ANTE-ROOM – DAY

Susan creeps up the stairs, one hand on the hilt of the
sword.

She can hear voices above her. She peers
over the edge of the stairwell.

Below she can Sideney working on the
door in one curved wall. Banjo is stood
over him . . .

She starts to move her hand but Teatime
is there first, dragging the sword
scabbard out of her belt.

Susan turns her head slowly.

It's Teatime.

> TEATIME

> (cheerful)
> Hello.

> TEATIME
> Well, well, well, what have we
> here? Bone handle, rather
> tasteless skull and bone
> decoration . . . Death himself's
> second favourite weapon, am I right?
> Oh, my! It must be Hogswatch! And
> this must mean that you are Susan,
> the famous granddaughter. Nobility.
> I'd bow . . .

He dances back and forces her into the room
with the sword.

INT. TOOTH FAIRY'S CASTLE/TOOTH FAIRY'S ANTE-ROOM - DAY

Susan backs into the room.

> **TEATIME**
> . . . but I'm afraid you'd do
> something dreadful.

There is a click, and a little gasp of
excitement from the wizard working on the door.

> **MR SIDENEY**
> Yes! Yes! Left-handed using a wooden
> pick! It's so simple!

He sees that even Susan is looking at him, and
coughs nervously.

> **MR SIDENEY (O.C.)**
> Ah, Mister Teatime, I've
> managed to open the fifth
> lock! No problem. They're just
> based on Woodeley's occult
> sequence.

Teatime doesn't take his eyes off Susan.

> **SUSAN**
> How do you know who I am?

> **TEATIME**
> Easy, Twurp's Peerage. Family
> motto: Non temetis messor.
> Your father was well known.
> Went a long way very fast. As
> for your grandfather . . .
> honestly, that motto,'Fear
> Not the Reaper . . .' Is that
> good taste? Of course, you
> don't need to fear him, do
> you? Or do you?

> **SUSAN**
> I don't know what you're
> talking about. Who are you,
> anyway?

> **TEATIME**
> I beg your pardon. My name is
> Teh-ah-time-eh, Jonathan Teh-
> ah-time-eh. At your service.

200

                              SUSAN
              You mean . . . like around four o'clock
              in the afternoon?

                            TEATIME
              No. I did say Teh-ah-time-eh. Please
              don't try to break my concentration by
              annoying me. How are you getting on, Mr
              Sideney?

                          MR SIDENEY
              Um . . . very well.

                            TEATIME
              If it's just according to Woodeley's
              sequence, number six should be copper
              and blue-green light.

He still doesn't break her gaze.

                            TEATIME
              Do you think your grandfather will try
              to rescue you? But now I have his
              sword, you see. I wonder . . .

There is the *snickersnicker* sound of scissors from
outside the door. Sideney jumps and fumbles at the
lock.

                            TEATIME
              All fingers and thumbs, Mr Sideney?

There is another click.

                          MR SIDENEY
              I've managed to open the sixth lock,
              Mister Teatime!

                            TEATIME
              Really. But it may not be all important
              now. Thank you, anyway. You've been
              most helpful.

                          MR SIDENEY
              Er . . .

                            TEATIME
              Yes, you may go.

Sideney doesn't even bother to pick up his books and
tools, but runs out of the room as fast as he can.

SUSAN
Is that all you're here for? A
robbery? Like a petty thief?

Teatime dances excitedly.

TEATIME
A thief? Me? I'm not a thief,
madam.

Medium Dave hurries into the room.

Teatime gestures to Medium Dave.

TEATIME
No, these gentlemen are thieves.
That's Medium Dave and exhibit B
is Banjo. He can talk.

Medium Dave nods at Susan. She sees the
look in his eyes. Maybe there is
something she can use . . .

INT. TOOTH FAIRY'S CASTLE/STAIRS – DAY

Sideney doesn't look back as he scurries
down the stairs and . . . bumps into Bilious and Violet
moving much more slowly.

MR SIDENEY
Uh!

He pushes past them.

VIOLET
Who are you?

MR SIDENEY
I'm . . . incognito.

Sideney disappears down the stairs in front of them.

VIOLET
Looked like a wizard to me.

And then Sideney is suddenly running back up towards
them.

Shaking like a leaf, Bilious stands in front of Violet,
as if to defend her.

Sideney freezes on the spot.

Convinced he's had this heroic effect, Bilious puffs his chest. He's about to speak when just out of the corner of his eye he sees something move on the stairs on the opposite side of the shaft . . . it flashes like metal blades catching the light.

Sideney gasps and stares at the opposite stairs. His thumb rises to his mouth as he turns and stares at Bilious. In the distance we can hear the faint sound of snipping.

> VIOLET
> (innocently)
> Did you suck your thumb when
> you were little?

Sideney pulls his thumb quickly from his mouth.

> MR SIDENEY

No!

Bilious looks behind Sideney and points.

> BILIOUS
> (really interested)
> Is that the Scissor Man . . .

> MR SIDENEY
> Shutupshutupshutupshutupshutupshutup!

Sideney shuts his eyes.

Violet grabs Bilious and waves frantically towards the bottom of the stairs.

> MR SIDENEY
> Kids believe all kinds of crap! But I'm
> grown up now . . .

Bilious and Violet hurry away.

Sideney's eyes are shut tight. The *snip, snip* sound snickers again. It sounds very close now. The camera closes in on Mr Sideney's hat and we hear his screams.

The *snickersnicker* of the SCISSOR MAN's thousand blades
is deafening.

INT. TOOTH FAIRY'S CASTLE/TOOTH FAIRY'S ANTE-ROOM – DAY

Teatime stares at Susan and then suddenly is much
closer.

                    TEATIME
          No more Hogfather. And that's only the
          start. I'll be able to make people
          believe anything I want.

There is a rumble like an avalanche, a long way off.
The dormant Banjo has awakened. His enormous hands
start to bunch.

                    BANJO
          What's dis? You said no more Hogfather.

He stands, like a mountain range.

Teatime stares at him and then glances at Medium Dave.

                    TEATIME
          He does know what we've been doing,
          doesn't he? You did tell him?

Medium Dave shrugs.

                    BANJO
          Dere's got to be a Hogfather. Dere's
          always a Hogfather.

Susan looks down. Grey blotches are speeding across the
white marble. She is standing in a pool of grey. So is
Banjo. And around Teatime the dots bounce and recoil
like wasps around a pot of jam.

Teatime points at Susan.

                    TEATIME
          She did it. She killed him.

The sheer playground effrontery of it shocks Susan.

                    SUSAN
          No I didn't. He—

                    TEATIME
          Did!

                         SUSAN
          Didn't!

                         TEATIME
          Did!

                         SUSAN
          Didn't!

                         TEATIME
          Did!

Banjo's big bald head turns towards her.

                         BANJO
          What's dis about the Hogfather?

                         SUSAN
          I don't think he's dead. But Teatime
          has made him very ill . . .

                         TEATIME
          Who cares? When this is over, Banjo,
          you'll have as many presents as you
          want. Trust me!

                         BANJO
          Dere has to be a Hogfather. Else dere's
          no Hogswatch.

                         TEATIME
          It's just another solar festival.

Medium Dave confronts Teatime. He has his hand on his
sword.

                         MEDIUM DAVE
          Banjo and me are going. Banjo? You're
          coming with me right now!

Teatime points to Susan.

                         TEATIME
          Grab her, Banjo. It's all her fault!

Banjo lumbers a few steps in Susan's direction, and
then stops.

                         BANJO
          Our mam said no hittin' girls. No
          touchin' 'em. No pullin' 'm hair . . .

Teatime rolls his one good eye.

                         TEATIME
              She's not a girl . . .

He stares at Susan.

                         TEATIME
              . . . she's a freak.

Susan stares at him.

Around his feet the greyness seems to be boiling in the
stone, following his feet as they move. And it is
around Banjo, too.

                         SUSAN
                (sweetly)
              I think I know you, Teatime. You're the
              mad kid they're all scared of, right?

                         TEATIME
              Banjo? I said grab her . . .

                         BANJO
              Our mam said . . .

                         SUSAN
              The kid who didn't know the
              difference between chucking a
              stone at a cat and setting it
              on fire.

To her delight he glares at her.

                         TEATIME
              I said shut up! Get her, Banjo!

There is a touch of vibrato in Teatime's
voice that hasn't been there before.

                         SUSAN
              The kind of little boy . . . who
              looks up dolls' dresses . . .

                         TEATIME
              I didn't!

Banjo looks worried.

                         BANJO
              Our mam said . . .

                         TEATIME
             Oh, to blazes with your mam!

There is a whisper of steel as Medium Dave draws his
sword.

                      MEDIUM DAVE
             What's that about our mam?

Now Teatime's having to concentrate on three people.

                         SUSAN
             I bet no one wanted to play with you.
             Not the kid with no friends.

                        TEATIME
               (faltering)
             Banjo! You do as I tell you!

The monstrous man is beside her now. His face is
twisted in an agony of indecision. His enormous fists
clench and unclench.

                         BANjo
             Our mam . . . Our mam . . . Our mam
             said . . .

The grey marks flow across the floor and form a pool of
shadow which grows darker and higher with astonishing
speed. It towers over the three men, and grows a shape.

                   MA LILYWHITE (V.O.)
             Have you been a bad boy, Banjo?

The huge woman towers over all three men. In one meaty
hand it is holding a bundle of birch twigs as thick as
a man's arm. The thing growls.

Medium Dave looks up into the enormous face of MA
LILYWHITE. Every pore is a pothole. Every brown tooth
is a tombstone.

                   MA LILYWHITE (V.O.)
             You been letting him get into trouble,
             our Davey? You have, ain't you?

He backs away.

                      MEDIUM DAVE
             No, Mum . . . no, Mum . . . no, Mum!

                    MA LILYWHITE (V.O.)
          You need a good hiding, Banjo?

                         BANJO
          Sorry. Sorry, sorry, Mum.

                    MA LILYWHITE
          You been playing with girls again?

Banjo sags on to his knees, tears of misery rolling
down his face.

                         BANJO
            Sorry Mum sorry sorry Mum noooohhh Mum
            sorry Mum sorry sorry . . .

Then the figure turns to Medium Dave again.

The sword drops out of his hand. His face seems to
melt. Medium Dave starts to cry.

                    MEDIUM DAVE
          No Mum no Mum no Mum nooooh Mum . . .

He gives a gurgle and collapses, clutching his chest.
And vanishes.

Teatime starts to laugh.

Susan taps him on the shoulder and as he looks round,
hits him as hard as she can across the face.

But . . . his hand moves faster and catches her wrist.
It is like striking an iron bar.

                       TEATIME
          Oh, no. I don't think so.

Out of the corner of her eye, Susan sees Banjo crawling
across the floor to where his brother had been. Ma
Lilywhite has vanished.

                       TEATIME
          This place gets into your head, doesn't
          it? It finds out how to deal with you.
          But I'm in touch with my inner child.

He reaches out with his other hand and grabs her hair,
pulling her head back.

                    TEATIME
          (whispering)
     And it's so much more fun.

Susan feels his grip lessen. There's a wet thump like a
piece of steak hitting a slab and Teatime goes past
her, on his back.

                    BANJO
     No pullin' girls' hair. That's
     bad.

Teatime bounces up like an acrobat
and steadies himself on the
railing of the stairwell. Then he
draws the sword. The blade is
invisible in the bright light of
the tower.

                    TEATIME
     I'm going to have such
     fun with this.

He waves it at them.

                    TEATIME
     It's so light.

                    SUSAN
     You wouldn't dare use it. My
     grandfather will come after
     you.

She walks towards him. She sees one
eye twitch.

                    TEATIME
     He comes after everyone.

                    SUSAN
     He's very singleminded.

Susan is much closer now.

                    TEATIME
     I'll be ready for him.

He brings the sword around. She doesn't even have time
to duck. And doesn't even try to when he swings the
sword back again. Teatime drops the sword to the floor
below.

                         SUSAN
          It doesn't work here. There's no Death
          here!

She slaps him across the face.

                         SUSAN
            (brightly)
          Hi, Inner Child! I'm the Inner
          Babysitter!

She doesn't punch. She just thrusts out an arm, palm
first, catching him under the chin and lifting him
backwards over the rail.

He somersaults . . . and somehow manages with his free
arm to grab at hers.

Susan's feet come off the ground, and she is over the
rail. She catches it with her other hand.

Teatime swings from her arm, staring upwards with a
thoughtful expression as Susan loses her grip, and just
catches a tooth-shaped decoration below.

The cloth of her sleeve begins to tear and the dress
rips.

For an instant he holds on to nothing and then, still
wearing the expression of someone trying to solve a
complex problem, he falls away, spinning, getting
smaller . . .

INT. UNSEEN UNIVERSITY/GREAT HALL - NIGHT

                         RIDCULLY
          Happy Hogswatch!

The Bursar sits nervously amid the cacophony of wizards
in full-on banquet mode. He eyes the nearest roast pig
with nervous anticipation. He tucks his napkin firmly
under his chin and raises a large fork.

There is a sound like coarse fabric ripping, somewhere
in the air in front of the Bursar, and a crash as
something lands on top of the roast pig. Roast potatoes
and gravy fill the air. The apple that had been in the
pig's mouth is violently expelled and hits the Bursar
on the forehead.

He blinks, looks down, and finds he is about to plunge his fork into a human head.

                    BURSAR
          (murmuring)
     Ahaha.

The wizards heave aside the overturned dishes and smashed crockery.

               LECTURER IN RECENT RUNES
     Is he dead?

Ponder puts his ear to the fallen man's chest.

                PONDER STIBBONS
     He's not breathing!

            CHAIR OF INDEFINITE STUDIES
     Breathing spell, breathing spell. Er
     . . . Spolt's Forthright Respirator,
     perhaps? I think I've got it written
     down somewhere . . .

Ridcully reaches through the wizards and pulls out the black-clad man by a leg. He holds him upside down in his big hand and thumps him heavily on the back.

The corpse makes a noise somewhere between a choke and a cough.

                    RIDCULLY
     Come on you chaps, give me some space.

The Archchancellor clears an area of table with one sweep of his spare arm.

The corpse opens his eyes. It's TEATIME.

He has a very close-up view of Ridcully's nose.

                PONDER STIBBONS
     Excuse me, excuse me.

Ponder leans over with his notebook open.

                PONDER STIBBONS
     This is vitally important for the
     advancement of natural philosophy.
     Did you see any bright lights? Was

there a shining tunnel? Did you
see . . . did . . .

Ridcully pulls him away.

                    RIDCULLY
          What's all this, Mr Stibbons? Put the
          damned quill away.

                    TEATIME
          This must be Unseen University? And
          you're all wizards?

Teatime has risen on his elbows.

                    TEATIME
          There was a sword.

                    THE DEAN
          Oh yes, it's fallen on the floor.

The Dean reaches down.

                    THE DEAN
          Oh.

The wizards look at the large curved slice
of table falling away. Something has cut
through everything: wood, cloth, plates,
cutlery, food.

                    THE DEAN
          Did I do that?

The Dean raises his hand. The other wizards
scatter.

Teatime takes the sword-hilt from him.

                    TEATIME
          I really must be off.

He runs from the hall.

          LECTURER IN RECENT RUNES
          Well he won't get far. The main
          doors are locked in accordance with
          Archchancellor Spode's Rules.

RIDCULLY
Won't get far?

LECTURER IN RECENT RUNES
No.

RIDCULLY
While holding a sword that appears to
be able to cut through anything.

There is the sound of falling wood.

INT. TOOTH FAIRY'S CASTLE/BALCONY BY ANTE-ROOM – NIGHT

A hand like a bunch of bananas pulls
Susan back over the rail.

BANJO
You can get into trouble,
hittin' girls. No playin'
with girls.

BANJO
Wot am I gonna do now?

She stares at his big, tear-stained
face. She pulls a handkerchief out of
her pocket, dabs it over the worst
parts, helps him blow his nose, and
then tucks it into his hand.

Susan watches him plod off.

There is a click behind them. Gears
turn.

The door swings open. Cold white mist rolls out across
the floor.

She looks at the open doorway.

INT. TOOTH FAIRY'S CASTLE/WHITE ROOM – DAY

The room beyond the door is entirely white. The mist
that swirls at knee-level deadens even the sound of her
footsteps.

There is just a large four-poster bed, old and dusty,
and lying among the mounds of pillows is a frail OLD

LADY in a mob-cap. The old woman turns her head and
smiles at Susan.

> TOOTH FAIRY
> Hello, my dear.

Susan looks at the picture-perfect
patchwork quilt.

> SUSAN
> No.

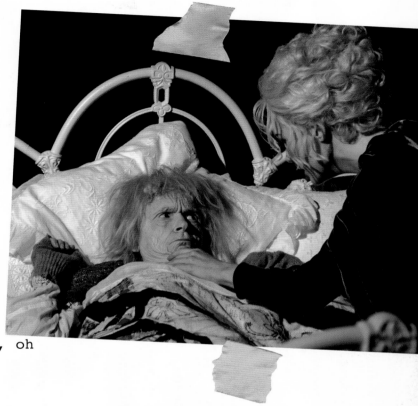

> TOOTH FAIRY
> Sorry, dear?

> SUSAN
> You're not the Tooth Fairy.

> TOOTH FAIRY
> Oh, I am, dear.

> SUSAN
> Oh, Grandma, what big teeth
> you have
> . . . You've even got a shawl, oh
> dear.

> TOOTH FAIRY
> I don't understand, lovey . . .

> SUSAN
> You forgot the rocking chair. I always
> thought there'd be a rocking
> chair . . .

Susan moves closer to her.

> SUSAN
> I don't think you're real. It's not
> a little old woman in a shawl
> running this place. You're out of my
> head. That's how you defend
> yourself . . . That's how you defend
> yourself. You poke around in people's
> heads and find the things that work—

The old woman changes into a jelly-like blob with a
terrible grin.

> SUSAN
> Nope. It's horrible, but it doesn't
> frighten me.

Then she turns into a spider, then a dog
and a rat.

              SUSAN
    I like spiders. Dogs? No. I like
    rats. Rats are fine,

A screaming monster face.

              SUSAN
    Sorry, is anyone frightened of
    that?

She grabs at the thing and this time the
shape stays. It is a small, wizened old
woman. Her hair is grey and lank. She
struggles weakly in Susans grasp, and
wheezes.

           THE BOGEYMAN
   I . . . I . . .

The Bogeyman hangs limp. She lets it down
again.

             SUSAN
    You're a Bogeyman, aren't you?

It collapses in a heap when she takes her
hand away.

           THE BOGEYMAN
    . . . not a . . . the . . .

             SUSAN
   The first Bogeyman?

And she sees how rangy it is, how white- and
grey-streaked its hair, how the skin is
stretched over the bones . . .

             SUSAN
  You look terrible.

           THE BOGEYMAN
  . . . thank you very much . . .

             SUSAN
  I mean ill.

Susan sits down on the bed.

                    THE BOGEYMAN
        I used to jump out on them and say
        'boo!'. But then I got to like 'em.
        Only children were frightened of me. I
        mean, what's to be scared of? Horns,
        bony arms . . .

She waves them unconvincingly.

                    THE BOGEYMAN
        But then I discovered that there were
        much worse things than me and I wanted
        to protect the children, keep them safe
        from all the really bad things. So I
        built all this to be a safe place.

Susan tries not to shudder.

                    SUSAN
        And the teeth?

                    THE BOGEYMAN
        Oh, if you leave all those teeth around
        anything could happen . . .

                    SUSAN
        Anything nearly did.

The Bogeyman starts to shake.

                    SUSAN
        So you are the Tooth Fairy, then?

                    THE BOGEYMAN
        Yes, I . . . and then they came . . .
        stealing . . . I'm too weak to look
        after them any more.

The Bogeyman groans.

                    THE BOGEYMAN
        . . . you don't die here. Just get
        old, listening to the laughter . . .

Susan nods. Faintly we can hear the distant chatter of
children.

                    SUSAN
        Don't worry about the teeth. I'll make
        them safe again.

The Bogeyman fades.

INT. TOOTH FAIRY'S CASTLE/FOOT OF TOWER - DAY

Banjo has a BROOM and MOP. The circle is empty and he is carefully washing the chalk away.

Susan comes down the steps and goes over to him.

> SUSAN
> I think it would be a good idea if you did the Tooth Fairy's job, Banjo.

> BANJO
> D'you . . . d'you think that'd be all right? Won't the Tooth Fairy mind?

> SUSAN
> You . . . do it until she comes back.

> BANJO
> So who's gonna tell me what to do?

> SUSAN
> No one's ever going to tell you what to do again, Banjo.

> BANJO
> Thanks. I will keep the teeth safe. Er, miss?

The big pink face looks at her.

> SUSAN
> Yes, Banjo?

> BANJO
> Can I have a puppy? I had a kitten once, but our mam drownded it 'cos it was dirty.

Susan thinks for a moment.

> SUSAN
> I think it'll turn up quite soon, Banjo.

> BANJO
> Thanks, miss.

Susan looks back up the tower, then turns to leave. Just as she does Bilious bursts in, followed by Violet. He is waving a branch like a club. He sees Banjo. He braces himself, closes his eyes and hurls himself towards him.

Susan watches as Bilious bounces off the giant figure
and lands flat on his back. He still tries to wave the
branch.

                    BILIOUS
          Violet talked about it and we thought
          we ought to come back and help.

Banjo reaches out a hand and smiles his gappy smile.

Now Bilious is really confused.

                    SUSAN
          It's okay. They're all gone.

Bilious is almost convinced.

                    SUSAN
          And Banjo needed a new job.

Bilious lowers the branch and takes Banjo's hand.

                    VIOLET
          That's funny. So does Bili.

Susan looks at the oh God. He gives her a pleading
look.

                    SUSAN
          Look, why don't you two make yourselves
          useful and help Banjo clear up this
          mess? He's . . . pretty much running
          the place now.

Violet laughs.

                    VIOLET
          But he's . . .

                    SUSAN
          He's in charge.

Bilious and Violet look into each other's eyes.

                    VIOLET
          We'd . . . love to help Banjo . . .
          together.

                    SUSAN
          Good. Have fun. Now I'm going home.

And with that she walks towards the door and opens
it . . .

> SUSAN
> This is a hell of a way to spend
> Hogswatch.

EXT. GAITER'S HOUSE - NIGHT

Binky walks towards the house.

Binky stops.

A skeletal hand grabs his bridle. DEATH materialises.

> SUSAN
> Grandfather. What are you doing here?

> DEATH
> IT IS NOT OVER.

Susan sags.

> DEATH
> YOU MUST BRING THE HOGFATHER HOME.

EXT. ICY MOUNTAINS - NIGHT

Binky, carrying DEATH and Susan, gallops through the
icy mountains.

The mists part. Sharp peaks are around them, lit by the

glow off the snow.

                    SUSAN
          These look like the mountains where the
          Castle of Bones was.

                    DEATH
          THEY ARE.

Binky canters low over the treetops.

Susan stares down out of sheer annoyance, and sees
something below.

                    SUSAN
           It's a pig!

                    DEATH
          A BOAR.

She sees movement against the snow, a blurred, dark
shape dodging and skidding and never clear: something
is being hunted.

Small dark shapes move across the whiteness, running in
pursuit.

Now they are lower she can see the hunters clearly.
They are large dogs. Their quarry is indistinct,
dodging among snowdrifts, keeping to the cover of snow-
laden bushes.

A drift explodes. Something big and long and blue-black
rises through the flying snow like a sounding whale.

She can hear the panting of the creature. The dogs make
no sound at all. Blood streams onto the snow from the
wounds they have already managed to inflict.

                    SUSAN
          This . . . boar is the . . .

                    DEATH
          YES. THE HOGFATHER AS HE BEGAN.

                    SUSAN
          And the dogs?

                    DEATH
          THESE ARE NOT REAL DOGS. IF THEY CATCH
          HIM, HE WON'T JUST DIE, HE WILL NEVER
          BE.

                              SUSAN
                 Well, stop them!

                              DEATH
                 THIS IS A HUMAN THING. THE AUDITORS ARE
                 DESPERATE NOW. THEY'RE DETERMINED TO
                 DESTROY THE HOGFATHER AT WHATEVER COST.
                 YOU MUST SAVE HIM.

DEATH nods his head towards the boar.

Binky is keeping level with it now, barely a few feet
away.

Realisation dawns on Susan's face. She glances ahead.
The snowfield has a cut-off look.

CAMERA on Susan's face.

Susan leaps. For a moment she floats through the air,
dress streaming behind her, arms outstretched . . .

And she lands on the animal's back. It stumbles for a
moment and then rights itself. Susan's arms cling to
its neck and her face is buried in its sharp bristles.
She scrunches up her nose from the stink of sweat, and
blood, and pig. And they flee from the dogs.

And suddenly there is a lack of landscape in front of
her.

The boar ploughs into the snow on the edge of the drop,
almost flinging her off, and turns to face the hounds.

There are four of them. And not the big floppy sort.

She rams her heels in and grabs a pig's ear in each
hand. She hauls them hard to one side.

To her amazement the boar grunts, prances on the lip of
the precipice and scrambles away.

The hounds flounder as they turn to follow skittering
feet along the edge of the plateau with its cavernous
drop.

The dogs are flying at the boar's heels again.

Susan looks around in the grey, sightless air for
somewhere, some way . . .

                               222

EXT. NARROW RIDGE – NIGHT

. . . and there is.

Ahead there is a shoulder of rock, a giant knife-edge
connecting this plain to the hills beyond like a narrow
foot-bridge. It is sharp, a thin line of snow with
chilly depths on either side.

The boar reaches the edge and hesitates. Susan puts her
head down and digs her heels in again.

Then, snout down, legs moving like pistons, the beast
plunges out onto the rock ridge. Snow sprays up as its
trotters seek for purchase.

A trotter slips.

The other feet scrabble at icy rock.

Susan flings herself the other way, clinging to the neck, and looks down to the dragging abyss under her feet.

There is nothing there.

Powdered ice makes her eyes sting. A flailing trotter almost slams against her head.

The creature's eye is inches away. It is as if someone is looking back at her . . .

A foot catches the rock.

Susan kicks herself upwards in one last effort.

Boar and woman rock for a moment and then a trotter catches a footing and the boar plunges forward along the ridge.

Susan risks a look behind.

The dogs are fast approaching the rock ridge.

Then suddenly another shock underfoot. Snow flies up.

Her world tilts . . .

The boar's muscles bunch as it leaps.

As its back legs leave the ground, a slab of ice and
rock comes away and begins the long slide into
darkness.

The dogs have reached the gap on the other side and are
milling round, struggling to prevent themselves
slipping.

The creature lands. Susan is thrown off and tumbles
into deep snow. She flails around madly.

Her hand finds a snow-encrusted branch.

A few feet away the boar lies on its side, steaming and
panting.

She pulls herself upright.

The spur here widens out into a hill, with a few frosted trees on it.

She puts both hands around the branch and heaves; it comes away with a crack, and she waves it like a club.

                    SUSAN
          Come on. Jump! Just
          you try it!

One does.

Susan spins and brings the branch round on the upswing, lifting the animal off its feet and out over the edge.

For a moment the shape wavers and then, howling, it drops out of sight.

She dances a few steps of rage and triumph.

                    SUSAN
       Yes! Yes! Who wants some? Anyone else?

The other dogs look her in the eye. They don't want any. And then they turn to see something blocking their retreat.

A FIGURE bars their way.

It seems to be made of snow, three balls of snow piled on one another. It has black dots for eyes. A semi-circle of more dots form the semblance of a mouth. There is a carrot for the nose.

And, for the arms, there appear to be two twigs . . . at this distance, anyway. One of the twigs is holding a long curved stick . . . A SCYTHE, in fact.

The dogs back away.

The snow breaks off the snowman in chunks, revealing a
gaunt figure in a flapping black robe.

                    DEATH
        HO. HO. HO.

The grey bodies smear and ripple as the hounds try
desperately to change their shape.

                    DEATH
            YOU COULDN'T RESIST IT IN THE END?

He touches the scythe. There is a click as the blade
flashes into life.

                    DEATH
        A MISTAKE, I FANCY.

DEATH steps forward.

                        DEATH
      IT GETS UNDER YOUR SKIN, LIFE. SPEAKING
      METAPHORICALLY, OF COURSE.

A dog starts to slip on the snow and scrabbles
desperately to save itself from the long, cold drop.

                        DEATH
      AND, YOU SEE, THE MORE YOU STRUGGLE FOR
      EVERY MOMENT, THE MORE ALIVE YOU STAY
      . . . WHICH IS WHERE I COME IN, AS A
      MATTER OF FACT.

The leading dog manages, for a moment, to become a grey
figure and manages to speak.

                      AUDITOR 2
      You cannot do this; there are rules!

                        DEATH
      YES. THERE ARE RULES. BUT YOU BROKE
      THEM. HOW DARE YOU? HOW DARE YOU?

The Auditor falls back into his dog shape.

The scythe blade is a thin blue outline in the grey
light.

DEATH raises a thin finger to where his lips might have
been and suddenly looks thoughtful.

                        DEATH
      AND NOW THERE REMAINS ONLY ONE FINAL
      QUESTION.

He raises his hands. Light flares in his eye-sockets.
As he speaks, avalanches fall in the mountains.

                        DEATH
      HAVE YOU BEEN NAUGHTY . . . OR NICE?

There is a deathly pause.

                        DEATH
      HO. HO. HO.

Susan hears the wails die away.

The boar lies in white snow that is now red with blood.
She kneels down and tries to lift its head.

It is dead. One eye stares at nothing. The tongue
lolls.

Sobs well up inside her.

                    SUSAN
       We saved you! Dying is not how it's
       supposed to go!

She drums on its flank with both fists.

A breeze blows up.

Something stirs in the landscape, something under the
snow. Tree branches shake gently, dislodging tiny
needles of ice.

The SUN rises.

The light streams over Susan like a silent gale. It is
dazzling. She crouches back, raising her forearm to
cover her eyes. The great red ball turns frost to fire
along the winter branches.

There is a groan.

A MAN lies in the snow where the boar had been. He is naked except for an animal skin loincloth. He is tattooed, blue whorls and spirals haunt his skin. He opens his eyes and stares at the sky.

Cold light slams into the mountain peaks, making every one a blinding, silent volcano. It rolls onwards, gushing into the valleys and thundering up the slopes, unstoppable . . .

The man heaves himself unsteadily to his feet, then slowly raises his arms and, silhouetted, greets the RISING SUN.

EXT. FOREST EDGE - DAWN

Four huge boars stand and steam, in front of the Hogfather's sleigh.

The Hogfather approaches. He seems almost to put on weight in the last few yards. He climbs aboard and sits down. It is almost impossible to see anything other than the huge, red-robed man, ice crystals settling here and there on the cloth. Only occasionally is there a hint of hair or tusk.

He shifts on the seat and then reaches down to extricate a false beard, which he holds up questioningly.

                    DEATH
    OH, ER, SORRY.

The Hogfather nods at DEATH and then at Susan. Is it thanks?

Then he shakes the reins and shouts and the sleigh slides away.

DEATH and Susan watch it go.

Now the Hogfather is a red dot on the other side of the valley.

> SUSAN
>
> Well, that about wraps it up for this dress. I'd just like to ask, purely out of academic interest . . . you were sure I was going to survive, were you?

> DEATH
>
> I WAS QUITE CONFIDENT.

> SUSAN
>
> Good.

There is a pause in the conversation.

> SUSAN
>
> Now . . . tell me—

> DEATH
>
> WHAT WOULD HAVE HAPPENED IF YOU HADN'T SAVED HIM?

> SUSAN
>
> Yes!

> DEATH
>
> THE SUN WOULD NOT HAVE RISEN.

> SUSAN
>
> Then what would have happened?

> DEATH
>
> A MERE BALL OF FLAMING GAS WOULD HAVE ILLUMINATED THE WORLD.

They walk in silence for a moment.

> SUSAN
>
> All right, I'm not stupid. You're saying that humans need . . . fantasies to make life bearable.

DEATH
NO. HUMANS NEED FANTASY TO BE HUMAN. TO
BE THE PLACE WHERE THE FALLING ANGEL
MEETS THE RISING APE.

SUSAN
With Tooth Fairies? Hogfathers?

DEATH
YES. AS PRACTISE. YOU HAVE TO START OUT
LEARNING TO BELIEVE THE LITTLE LIES.

SUSAN
So we can believe the big ones?

DEATH
YES. JUSTICE. MERCY. DUTY. THAT SORT OF
THING.

SUSAN
They're not the same at all!

DEATH
YOU THINK SO? THEN TAKE THE UNIVERSE
AND GRIND IT DOWN TO THE FINEST POWDER
AND SIEVE IT THROUGH THE FINEST SIEVE
AND THEN SHOW ME ONE ATOM OF JUSTICE,
ONE MOLECULE OF MERCY. AND YET . . .

DEATH waves a hand.

                                    DEATH
                          . . . YOU TRY TO ACT AS IF
                          THERE IS SOME IDEAL ORDER IN
                          THE WORLD, AS IF THERE IS
                          SOME . . . SOME RIGHTNESS IN
                          THE UNIVERSE BY WHICH IT MAY BE
                          JUDGED.

                                    SUSAN
                          But people have got to believe
                          that, or what's the point . . .
                          ?

                                    DEATH
                          YOU NEED TO BELIEVE IN THINGS
                          THAT AREN'T TRUE. HOW ELSE CAN
                          THEY BECOME?

EXT. GAITER'S HOUSE – DAY

Binky trots to a standstill outside the house. Susan
climbs down onto the fresh snow. As her boot lands it
MORPHS back into her Governess shoes.

Her hair and clothes are all back to normal as she
stands uncertainly for a moment.

> DEATH
> (hopeful)
> ER . . . WOULD YOU LIKE TO VISIT FOR
> HOGSWATCH DINNER? ALBERT IS FRYING A
> PUDDING.

> SUSAN
> I . . . er . . . well they're really
> expecting me here.

DEATH nods in an understanding way.

> SUSAN
> Would you like a drink before you go?

> DEATH
> A CUP OF COCOA WOULD BE APPROPRIATE IN
> THE CIRCUMSTANCES.

INT. GAITER'S HOUSE/NURSERY – DAY

Susan takes her coat off.

> SUSAN
> Right. There are biscuits in the tin on
> the mantelpiece.

Susan heads with relief into the tiny kitchen.

DEATH helps himself to a biscuit from the tin. There
are two full stockings hanging from the mantelpiece. He
prods them with professional satisfaction. He picks up
a HOGSWATCH CARD. It is fully back to normal. The
HOGFATHER is the Hogfather once more.

DEATH sits down in the creaking wicker chair, buries
his feet in the rug and looks around with interest. He
hears the clatter of cups, and then a sound like
indrawn breath, and then silence.

His gaze travels to the door. Susan's Governess coat
and hat are hanging on it.

The door opens.

To his horror, DEATH sees a small CHILD of unidentifiable sex come out of the bedroom, amble sleepily across the floor and unhook the stockings from the mantelpiece. It is halfway back before it notices him and then it simply stops and regards him thoughtfully.

                    TWYLA
        Susan's gotta poker, you know.

                    DEATH
        MY GOODNESS ME.

                    TWYLA
        I fort all of you knew that now.

                    DEATH
        INDEED.

                    TWYLA
        Larst week she picked a Bogey up by
        its nose.

DEATH is for once speechless.

                    TWYLA
        I'll give Gawain his stocking and then
        I'll come an' watch.

The child pads out. DEATH looks to the kitchen.

                    DEATH
        SUSAN?

Susan comes out of the kitchen, a kettle in her hand.

There is a figure behind her. In the half-light the sword gleams blue along its blade.

Its glitter reflects off one glass eye.

                    TEATIME
        Well, well, now this is unexpected. A
        family affair?

The sword hums back and forth.

                    TEATIME
        I wonder? Is it possible to kill Death?
        Mmm, this must be a very special
        sword, . . .

He beheads a wooden toy.

>   TEATIME
> And it certainly works
> here . . . and of course it
> might well not be regarded as
> murder. Possibly it is a civic
> act. It would be, as they say,
> The Big One. You may have some
> personal knowledge about your
> vulnerability, but I'm pretty
> certain that Susan here would
> quite definitely die, so I'd
> rather you didn't try any last-
> minute stuff.

>   DEATH
> I AM LAST-MINUTE STUFF.

DEATH stands up.

Teatime circles around carefully, the sword's tip making little curves in the air.

From the next room comes the sound of someone trying to blow a whistle quietly.

Susan glances at her grandfather.

>   SUSAN
> I don't remember them asking for
> anything that made a noise.

>   DEATH
> OH, THERE HAS TO BE SOMETHING IN THE
> STOCKING THAT MAKES A NOISE. OTHERWISE
> WHAT IS 4.30 A.M. FOR?

>   TEATIME
> There are children? Oh yes, of course.
> Call them.

>   SUSAN
> Certainly not!

>   TEATIME
> It will be instructive. Educational.
> And when your adversary is Death, you
> cannot help but be the good guy.

He points the sword at Susan.

                    TEATIME
          Call them.

Susan glances hopefully at her grandfather.

He nods. For a moment a glow in one eye-socket flickers
off and on, DEATH's equivalent of a wink.

                    SUSAN
          Gawain? Twyla?

The muffled noises stop in the next room. There is a
padding of feet and two solemn faces appear round the
door.

                    TEATIME
          (genially)
            Come in, come in, curly-haired tots.

Gawain gives him a steely stare.

                    TEATIME
          I caught this Bogeyman. What
          shall we do with him, eh?

The two faces turn to DEATH. Twyla puts
her thumb in her mouth.

                    GAWAIN
                 (critically)
          It's only a skeleton.

Susan opens her mouth, and the sword
swings towards her. She shuts it again.

                    TEATIME
           Yes, a nasty, creepy, horrible
           skeleton. Scary, eh?

There is a very faint 'pop' as Twyla
takes her thumb out of her mouth.

                    TWYLA
          He's eating a bittit.

Susan starts to swing the kettle in an absentminded
way.

                    TEATIME
          A creepy bony man in a black robe!

He spins round to face Susan.

                    TEATIME
          You're fidgeting with that kettle. So I
          expect you're thinking of doing
          something creative. Put it down,
          please. Slowly.

Susan gently and puts the kettle on a chair.

                    GAWAIN
          Huh, that's not very creepy, it's just
          bones. It's just standing there. It's
          not even making woo-woo noises. And
          anyway, you're creepy. Your eye's
          weird.

                    TEATIME
          Really? Then let's see how creepy I can
          be.

Blue fire crackles along the sword as he raises it.

Susan closes her hand over the poker.

Teatime sees her start to turn. He steps behind DEATH,
sword raised . . .

Susan throws the poker over-arm. It makes a ripping
noise as it shoots through the air, and trails sparks.

It hits DEATH's robe and vanishes. He blinks.

Teatime smiles at Susan. He turns and peers dreamily at
the sword in his hand.

It falls out of his fingers.

DEATH turns and catches it by the handle as it tumbles,
and turns its fall into an upward curve.

Teatime looks down at the poker in his chest as he
folds up. Blood trickles from one eye and tears from
the other.

                    TEATIME
          Oh, no. It couldn't have gone through
          you. There's so many ribs and things!

                    TWYLA
          It only kills monsters.

                    SUSAN
          Stop time now.

DEATH snaps his fingers. The room takes on the greyish
purple of stationary time. The clock pauses its
ticking.

                    SUSAN
          You winked at me! I thought you had a
          plan!

                    DEATH
          INDEED. OH, YES. I PLANNED TO SEE WHAT
          YOU WOULD DO.

                    SUSAN
          What?

                    DEATH
          I DID ADD THE SPARKLY STARS AND THE
          NOISE, THOUGH. I THOUGHT THEY WOULD BE
          APPROPRIATE.

                    SUSAN
          And if I hadn't done anything?

                    DEATH
          I DARESAY I WOULD HAVE THOUGHT OF
          SOMETHING. AT THE LAST MINUTE.

                    SUSAN
          That was the last minute!

                    DEATH
          THERE IS ALWAYS TIME FOR ANOTHER LAST
          MINUTE.

DEATH turns to the fallen Teatime.

                    DEATH
          STOP PLAYING DEAD, MISTER TEH-
          AH-TIME-EH.

The ghost of the Assassin springs up like a
Jack-in-the box, all slightly crazed smiles.

                    TEATIME
          He got it right!

                    DEATH
          OF COURSE.

Teatime begins to fade.

                    DEATH
          I'LL TAKE CARE OF THE BODY.
          THAT WILL PREVENT INCONVENIENT
          QUESTIONS.

                    DEATH
          ER . . . YOU DID KNOW THE POKER
          WOULD GO THROUGH ME?

Susan hesitates.

                    SUSAN
          I was quite confident.

                    DEATH
          AH.

Her grandfather stares at her for a moment and
then turns towards the balcony. And then he
seems to remember something else. He fumbles
inside his robe.

                    DEATH
          I HAVE MADE THIS FOR YOU.

She reaches out and takes a square of damp
cardboard. Water drips off the bottom. Somewhere
in the middle, a few brown feathers seemed to
have been glued on.

                    SUSAN
          Oh. Thank you. What is it?

                    245

DEATH
ALBERT SAID THERE OUGHT TO BE SNOW ON
IT, BUT IT APPEARS TO HAVE MELTED. IT
IS, OF COURSE, A HOGSWATCH CARD.

SUSAN
Oh . . .

DEATH
THERE SHOULD HAVE BEEN A ROBIN ON IT AS
WELL, BUT I HAD CONSIDERABLE DIFFICULTY
IN GETTING IT TO STAY ON.

SUSAN
Ah . . .

DEATH
IT WAS NOT AT ALL CO-OPERATIVE.

SUSAN
Really . . . ?

DEATH
IT DID NOT SEEM TO GET INTO THE
HOGSWATCH SPIRIT AT ALL.

SUSAN
Oh. Thank you.

She pauses for thought.

                        SUSAN
        Granddad?

                        DEATH
        YES?

                        SUSAN
        Why? I mean, why did you do all this?

He stands quite still for a moment.

                        DEATH
        HUMAN BEINGS MAKE LIFE SO INTERESTING.
        DO YOU KNOW THAT IN A UNIVERSE SO FULL
        OF WONDERS THEY HAVE MANAGED TO INVENT
        BOREDOM? QUITE ASTONISHING.

                        SUSAN
        Oh.

                        DEATH
        WELL THEN . . . HAPPY HOGSWATCH.

                        SUSAN
        Yes. Grandad? Happy Hogswatch.

Susan watches Death leave, and smiles.

DEATH pauses at the window.

                        DEATH
        HAPPY HOGSWATCH. AND GOOD NIGHT,
        CHILDREN . . . EVERYWHERE.

EXT. GAITER'S HOUSE/NURSERY - DAY

The CAMERA pulls back from DEATH looking out of the
window and up and away from the snow-covered
house . . .

INT. DEATH'S HOUSE - NIGHT

Albert is frying a pudding on a stove. He has a roll-up
in his mouth. He magics a flame on the end of his
finger and FINALLY lights the cigarette. He takes one
puff, coughs, and with a look of disgust throws it
away.

INT. TOOTH FAIRY'S CASTLE/FOOT OF TOWER - DAY

While clearing away teeth, BANJO sees a PUPPY.

> **BANJO**
> Ooh, hello. Hello, boy. You're cute. Ha
> ha. Yeah, come on. Come on, let's play!

INT. TOYMAKER'S SHOP - DAY

A long, long time ago . . . . the shop door opens. The
little TOYMAKER stops dead.

> **DEATH**
> YOU HAVE A BIG WOODEN ROCKING HORSE IN
> THE WINDOW.

> **TOYMAKER**
> Ah, yes, yes, yes. That's a . . .
> that's a special order made for Lord
> Rodney . . .

> **DEATH**
> HOW MUCH WOULD THIS LORDSHIP HAVE PAID
> YOU?

> **TOYMAKER**
> Twelve dollars.

> **DEATH**
> I WILL GIVE YOU FIFTY.

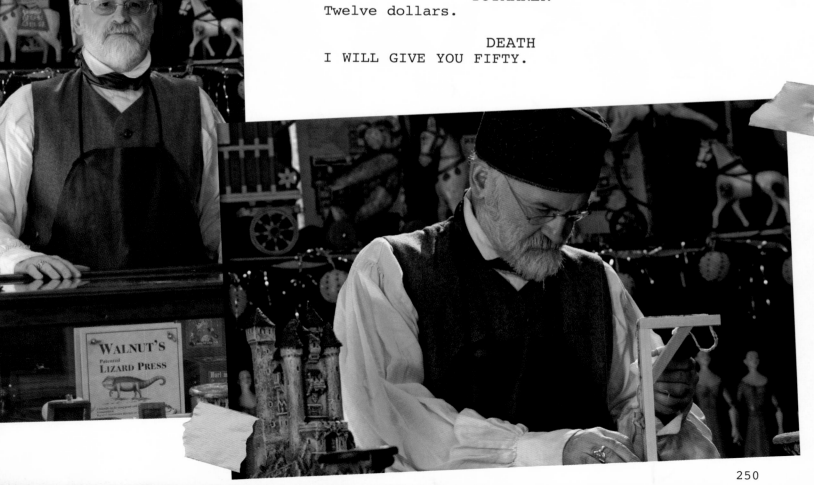

        TOYMAKER
    Would you like me to wrap it up for
    you, sir?

        DEATH
    NO. I WILL TAKE IT AS IT IS. THANK YOU

DEATH places a small clinking bag on the counter.

        DEATH
    INCIDENTALLY, THERE IS A SMALL BOY OUT
    THERE WITH HIS NOSE FROZEN TO THE
    WINDOW. SOME WARM WATER SHOULD DO THE
    TRICK.

And with that, DEATH leaves . . .

        TOYMAKER
    Happy Hoswatch, sir.

THE END

AFTERWORD

Bringing Discworld to life on the screen in the form of a live-action film for the very first time has been the most challenging and rewarding creative experiences of our lives. The enormity of what we were attempting really struck home from the very first moment that Terry allowed us the rights to adapt *Hogfather*, and again when we got the money in place from Sky and RHI to go ahead with filming. There are an enormous number of people we need to thank, for their help producing this landmark television film, most especially Terry himself, for being so supportive throughout the entire process, from writing to filming, and beyond.

Particular thanks go to the 'A list' creative and production team, not to mention the stellar cast who came to work with us at The Mob, all of whom put in long and arduous hours, well above the call of duty. Every single one of them strove to make their contribution the very best that it could possibly be, and it shows. We owe a huge debt of gratitude to all at BSkyB, James Murdoch, Dawn Airey, James Baker, Ian Lewis, Elaine Pyke et al, who had belief in the project to initially fund the development process and to support us into production. Thanks also to Richard Woolfe and Hannah Barnes for continuing to support the Franchise on Sky One. We also need to thank Robert Halmi Senior, Joel Denton and the RHI team in London and New York, our superb international partners.

And now on to the 'makers' of our film. There isn't space to thank everybody by name, but particular thanks must go to Vadim, for although he is a *Mobster* himself, and his vision, energy and enthusiasm usually know no bounds, he was put to the sternest test with us creating this film, and he came through with flying colours, doing a truly awesome job on all levels.

And special thanks also to Gavin Finney B.Sc. and his camera team who gave, through his inspired lighting, such a wonderfully Discworldy feel to the film; to Ricky Eyres for his brilliant set design, and to his props and construction team, who made – with far more creativity than money – some of the most wonderful and awe-inspiring sets and models ever seen on television (and on what was indeed a modest budget by Hollywood standards!). Jane Spicer and her team created wonderful costumes which really captured the mood, and Ros Peat's make-up design was as excellent as we've ever seen. Joe McNally's editing was truly inspired. The fact that they all *got* Discworld – even if they were new to Terry Pratchett's phenomenal world to start with – is what makes *Hogfather* so special.

While we're on the Big Thanks, we must mention Sean Glynn, our Line Producer, who created a fantastic spirit in the camp, and was a great wing man for us, despite the very tough schedule (and thanks for that to Pete Freeman, our dynamic first AD).

Heartfelt gratitude to Mark Benson and The Moving Picture Company, who have supported the project from concept forwards; they have invested a huge amount of time and resources into getting the project off the ground, and the special effects and creatures they designed for the film are truly wonderful.

Finally, we would be churlish indeed if we did not say hearty thanks to our families, who really haven't seen too much of us for the last two years; Kate and Pauline: all your patience and love have kept us going over the long production period.

We do so hope that you enjoy watching *Hogfather*, and we really look forward to turning more of the brilliant Discworld novels into movies in the future.

Rod Brown and Ian Sharples
Producers of Hogfather

P.S. Thanks also to Jo Fletcher of Victor Gollancz, for having the great idea of putting this book together, and for all the time and effort she and Nick May put into making it look so great!

THE CAST

MICHELLE DOCKERY	SUSAN
MARNIX VAN DEN BROEKE	DEATH
MARC WARREN	TEATIME
PETER GUINNESS	MEDIUM DAVE
STEPHEN MARCUS	BANJO
CRAIG CONWAY	CHICKENWIRE
NIGEL PLANER	MR SIDENEY
GEOFFREY HUTCHINS	MR BROWN
TERRY PRATCHETT	THE TOYMAKER
SIR DAVID JASON	ALBERT
JOSS ACKLAND	MUSTRUM RIDCULLY
ED COLEMAN	PONDER STIBBONS
JOHN FRANKLYN-ROBBINS	THE DEAN
ROGER FROST	THE BURSAR
TIMOTHY BATESON	LECTURER IN RECENT RUNES
JOHN BOSWALL	CHAIR OF INDEFINITE STUDIES
JAMES MELLOR	STUDENT WIZARD
TREVOR JONES	MODO
RHODRI MEILIR	BILIOUS
SINEAD MATTHEWS	VIOLET
DAVID WARNER	LORD DOWNEY
NICOLAS TENNANT	CORPORAL NOBBS
RICHARD KATZ	CONSTABLE VISIT
TONY ROBINSON	VERNON CRUMLEY
MARTHA KATZ	BOBBLE HAT CHILD
RACHEL EDWARDS	BOBBLE HAT CHILD'S MOTHER
DOMINIC BORELLI	GROTTO HOGFATHER
AARON BARKER	SMALL BOY
LYDIA ALTMAN	SMALL BOY'S SISTER
ROBERT PORTAL	MR GAITER
DEBORAH WINCKLES	MRS GAITER
MADELENE RAKIC-PLATT	TWYLA
HUGO ALTMAN	GAWAIN
JON RIDGEON	GUEST 1
SHEND	HOGFATHER
ARTHUR WHITE	ERNIE
FOX JACKSON-KEEN	YOUNG ALBERT
DON WETHERHEAD	SLIMAZEL THE BOGEYMAN
JOHN CARTIER	CARTER
JOHNNY WARMAN	TOOTHGUARD 1
TIM PLESTER	TOOTHGUARD 7
BRIDGET TURNER	TOOTHFAIRY / BOGEYMAN
GREGOR HENDERSON-BEGG	PIXIE HELPER
PETER HOLDWAY	AUDITOR 1
ANDRE LAMOTTE	AUDITOR 2
ADAM MARVEL	AUDITOR 3
ANDREW SWAIN	AUDITOR 4
DANNY DACOSTA	VERRUCA GNOME/HAIR LOSS FAIRY
KEN CAMPBELL	
MAGGIE McCARTHY	MA LILLYWHITE
NEIL PEARSON	RAVEN

and IAN RICHARDSON as the VOICE OF DEATH

Happy Hogswatch!